In The Net

By

Chuck Porte

Printed in the United States of America

Style Publishing
4356 Blackfoot Dr. SW
Grandville MI 49418
markvws@yahoo.com

Cover picture features a rainbow trout

Caught by Dan Sprys

on the

Frying Pan River in Colorado

November 17, 2022

Photo by Joe Sprys

Book Title

In the Net

Rendered by

John Dyksterhouse

Avid Christian

Excellent Fly Fisherman

In the Net

The meditations in this book are reflective of where one might be in relationship with your Maker and Redeemer. You are invited to picture yourself being attracted to, being drawn and eventually arriving in the net of the loving arms of Jesus.

The analogy is nautical and the similarity to becoming a Jesus follower and eventually being a born-again Christian is readily apparent. As you internalize the meditations within the ensuing pages may you visualize where you are presently at in your journey up the stream of life toward your eternal home with Jesus.

This Devotional takes passages from my 3 previous Devotionals: Devotions & Meditations, Between the Buoys, and Fish On. I selected devotionals that I thought would help people in their spiritual journey. If you care to leave me feedback, do not hesitate to email me at seaporte@sbcglobal.net

The Bible passages included are taken from the English Standard Version (ESV).

May the Lord Bless you through this devotional.

Table of Contents

A REST FOR THE PEOPLE OF GOD

7 Therefore, as the Holy Spirit says,
"Today, if you hear his voice,
8 do not harden your hearts as in the rebellion,
on the day of testing in the wilderness,
9 where your fathers put me to the test
and saw my works for forty years.
10 Therefore I was provoked with that generation,
and said, 'They always go astray in their heart;
they have not known my ways.'
11 As I swore in my wrath,
'They shall not enter my rest.'"
Hebrews 3:7-11

I for one have been super critical of the Israelites who grumbled and whined during the entire exodus toward the Promised Land. The author of Hebrews quotes directly from Psalm 95. We are led to believe that the book of Hebrews is probably directed to a Jewish population.

More than likely, only the children of the Israelites who began the exodus were led into the land of milk and honey. Forty years in the desert was a long time to be on a trek. If I were on that strenuous journey, I believe that I would have joined the others in complaining about the conditions, the heat, the lack of water, the same daily diet etc.

9

Our lives in some ways align with that of the Jews who were engaged on the exodus. We are all on a lifelong journey to a promised land. Our ultimate goal is to reach heaven at the end of our mortal existence. Along the way however, we experience difficulties and trials such as illness, accidents, pandemics, deaths of friends, family upsets, financial reversals, marital problems etc. The list goes on and on. In fact, we can conclude that our list of trials far exceeds that of the Jews on their exodus.

So where are you at in your journey toward your eternal rest? Are you sure that you are on the right path? Are you attempting to invite others to join you on your trek? When you experience difficulties are your words and actions depicting defeat or victory?

God closed the Promised Land to the Jews who were constantly grumbling and negative in all their actions. We will enter the eternal rest by grace but need to reflect that promise in all of our demeanor. Are you on board?

Prayer:
Father, we need to look at ourselves and ask forgiveness for any negativity in our attitudes. We will attempt to be more loving and more kind. In the name of Jesus, Amen

ABBA

HEIRS WITH CHRIST

[12] So then, brothers,[a] we are debtors, not to the flesh, to live according to the flesh. [13] For if you live according to the flesh you will die, but if by the Spirit you put to death the deeds of the body, you will live. [14] For all who are led by the Spirit of God are sons[b] of God. [15] For you did not receive the spirit of slavery to fall back into fear, but you have received the Spirit of adoption as sons, by whom we cry, "Abba! Father!" [16] The Spirit himself bears witness with our spirit that we are children of God, [17] and if children, then heirs—heirs of God and fellow heirs with Christ, provided we suffer with him in order that we may also be glorified with him.

Romans 8:12-17

A daughter of one of my closest friends has written an excellent book. She frequently used the word Abba to address God the Father. Abba is an Aramaic word for "Daddy". It is a name that has relationship and love built right into it. Her use of Abba tells me that her relationship with God is close and very personal.

11

In today's culture many have difficulty with being identified as children of a loving father. Many homes do not reflect the presence of a father and the children are being raised by a single mom. However, once we give our lives over to becoming followers of Jesus, we have received the spirit of adoption as children who have been chosen by God for eternal glory.

Now we can come to God the Father by addressing him as Abba. We are now his children, we are heirs, in fact, and we are co-heirs with Jesus.

The name Abba expresses intimacy with God the Father. Our God is a God of love rather than a harsh judge that condemns. In the role of heirs we will inherit all that God has promised. The ultimate reward as an heir is to spend eternity in the presence of God. In the meantime, our earthly journey continues with its joys and tears. Temptations remain, bills need to be paid, illness happens, jobs come and go etc. Life continues, but we are now on a path of glorification and it's eternal! We will spend eternity in a heaven beyond our imagination!

Where are you at with Jesus? Can you address the Father by calling him Abba?

Prayer:
Abba, Father, listen to your children praying. Give them the assurance that you have their backs, their hearts, in fact, their all. Amen

ARE WE THERE YET?

[16] "A little while, and you will see me no longer; and again a little while, and you will see me." [17] So some of his disciples said to one another, "What is this that he says to us, 'A little while, and you will not see me, and again a little while, and you will see me'; and, 'because I am going to the Father'?" [18] So they were saying, "What does he mean by 'a little while'? We do not know what he is talking about." [19] Jesus knew that they wanted to ask him, so he said to them, "Is this what you are asking yourselves, what I meant by saying, 'A little while and you will not see me, and again a little while and you will see me'? [20] Truly, truly, I say to you, you will weep and lament, but the world will rejoice. You will be sorrowful, but your sorrow will turn into joy.
John 16:16-20

Jesus is nearing the end of his visible ministry on earth. He is letting his disciples know that at his crucifixion he will vanish, and they won't see him again until after his resurrection. The second resurrection will be after his ascension. Only the Father knows when that will occur.

When Jesus comes again at the second resurrection we will all join in a throng of great rejoicing. Those who have died, their bodies will be resurrected. Those still alive will be part of a great transition from this earth to eternal glory.

The disciples are being educated by Jesus regarding the happenings to take place at the time of his death, burial and resurrection. Jesus explained that all this would take place "in a little while."

Today, we see a world in turmoil. America's society is doing whatever feels good and is living for their own pleasure. They are doing what is "right in their own eyes." Christians know that Jesus is coming again at the second resurrection and inwardly are asking the question, "are we there yet?" It is extremely important that every day we need to number our days as if Jesus is coming back today. Looking forward, it is a time of great rejoicing for faith filled Christians. For others, it is a time of denial and great fear.

Where are you as you consider the end of time on earth for all people? Are you prepared in that you have accepted Christ? You can make a decision for following Jesus right now by confessing your sins and promising to follow Jesus for the rest of your life. Jesus has paid the price for all your past, present and future sins by his crucifixion on the cross and through his resurrection from the dead three days later. We don't know if we are there yet but we know that we will join Jesus in heaven at the end of this earthly journey. The question that is always out there is "are we there yet?"

Prayer:

Heavenly Father, we don't know when Jesus is coming again. We know that this matter is totally only known by you. Erase my doubts that I might have and lift me from hope to assurance in faith. In Jesus holy name,

Amen

BALM IN GILEAD

¹⁸ My joy is gone; grief is upon me,
my heart is sick within me.
¹⁹ Behold, the cry of the daughter of my people
from the length and breadth of the land,
"Is the LORD not in Zion?
Is her King not in her?"
"Why have they provoked me to anger with their carved
images
and with their foreign idols?"
²⁰ "The harvest is past, the summer is ended,
and we are not saved."
²¹ For the wound of the daughter of my people is my
heart wounded;
I mourn, and dismay has taken hold on me.
²² Is there no balm in Gilead?
Is there no physician there?
Why then has the health of the daughter of my people
not been restored?
Jeremiah 8:18-22

The situation of the Jews at the time of Jeremiah's writing, was one of false confidence. They actually brought idolatry into the temple and worshipped Jehovah as just another god. The Jewish people were living in complacency. They figured that God would protect them and care for them, seeing that they were sort of worshipping God in close proximity to His holy temple.

God saw through their duplicity and directed Jeremiah to expose their false worship including their desecration of the temple.

The exiled Jews were forced to live in a far country. Being away from home gave birth to a cry of anguish, "is there no balm in Gilead"? Instead of turning to God they fled to some walled cities, Jeremiah cried out in anguish, and we hear God's voice in judgment, "Is there no balm in Gilead?"

African Americans in the midst of their former slave status caught the mood of angst and depression. African American, Howard Thurman reflects that the slaves caught the mood of despondency and changed it to a positive note to reflect that "there is a balm in Gilead." This became a positive exclamation of faith.

The spiritual "Balm in Gilead" has been immortalized by bass-baritone Paul Robeson (1896-1976) Later two operatic sopranos, Kathleen Battle 1948 and Jessye Norman 1945 continued the remembrance.

The Tuskegee Choir rendered a choral arrangement by William Levi Dawson (1899-1990). It is this arrangement that is most often sung by college, school and church choirs to this day.

America needs a Balm in Gilead to heal their sin-sick souls.

Prayer:

Father, often we feel our works in vain but then the Holy Spirit revives our soul again. Give us the courage and wisdom to tell the love of Jesus and proclaim, "He died for all". In Jesus holy name, Amen.

CALLED TO BE HOLY

[13] Therefore, preparing your minds for action, and being sober-minded, set your hope fully on the grace that will be brought to you at the revelation of Jesus Christ. [14] As obedient children, do not be conformed to the passions of your former ignorance, [15] but as he who called you is holy, you also be holy in all your conduct, [16] since it is written, "You shall be holy, for I am holy."
1 Peter 1:13-16

In the last few years, Lake Michigan has experienced extremely high-water levels. This phenomenon is part of a cycle where the great lakes water levels fluctuate from very low to very high because of snow melt and rainfall. When water levels are high, wind driven waves can destroy stairways leading to the beach and in many instances, homes are damaged or completely destroyed because of soil erosion caused by the sand bluffs being washed away by the high-water levels.

The analogy of rising water and sins connected to our former ignorance of God's law leads to gradual erosion of our earthly and spiritual footing. Erosion caused by high water levels is almost impossible to control. However the erosion of intentional sin when we know better is in direct violation of our expected behavior to be holy.

Are there alternate behaviors to God's command to "be holy"? Some alternates are:

Being holy only when others are watching
Being only as holy as my peers
Doing what is right in my own eyes

The apostle Peter was never known to speak to an issue in a delicate manner. He plainly says that our behavior is not to be the same as before (in our ignorance). In other words, once we have accepted Jesus' invitation to become a follower, our excuses for unholy actions and words cease to exist.

So why be holy? What is the goal? Simply put, our behavior in being holy is our way of saying "Thanks" to God for his great plan of salvation. Being holy will attract others by our holiness attempts. When the chariot arrives for your heaven bound journey, only tickets that are titled "Holiness" will be punched. Prepare your boarding pass!

Prayer:
Heavenly Father, thank you for your singular plan of salvation through your son Jesus Christ. May I grow in holiness as per your command? Amen

CHARIOT RIDE

⁶ Then Elijah said to him, "Please stay here, for the LORD has sent me to the Jordan." But he said, "As the LORD lives, and as you yourself live, I will not leave you." So the two of them went on. ⁷ Fifty men of the sons of the prophets also went and stood at some distance from them, as they both were standing by the Jordan. ⁸ Then Elijah took his cloak and rolled it up and struck the water, and the water was parted to the one side and to the other, till the two of them could go over on dry ground. ⁹ When they had crossed, Elijah said to Elisha, "Ask what I shall do for you, before I am taken from you." And Elisha said, "Please let there be a double portion of your spirit on me." ¹⁰ And he said, "You have asked a hard thing; yet, if you see me as I am being taken from you, it shall be so for you, but if you do not see me, it shall not be so." ¹¹ And as they still went on and talked, behold, chariots of fire and horses of fire separated the two of them. And Elijah went up by a whirlwind into heaven. ¹² And Elisha saw it and he cried, "My father, my father! The chariots of Israel and its horsemen!" And he saw him no more. Then he took hold of his own clothes and tore them in two pieces.
II Kings 2:6-12

Today's ultimate ride of celebration is a limo. It's not unusual for a limo to be used to carry a young man and his date to the high school prom. Heads of government are often conveyed to special meetings and/or banquets in a limo. In fact, for security reasons, the highest-level officers are transported in armor plated limos.

In the days of Elijah and Elisha a chariot was used primarily as a military conveyance. Chariots were also used as personal rides for high-ranking officers.

The transfer of power of biblical authority between the departing prophet Elijah to his assistant Elisha was of

19

significant importance. In fact, fifty sons of the prophets were in attendance as witnesses of the transfer of God's earthly leader of the Jewish people.

Elisha asked for a double portion of Elijah's spirit before Elijah was transported to eternal glory. As that conversation was still in progress, Elijah was surrounded by horses and chariots of fire. A mighty whirlwind whisked Elijah up into the heavens. Elisha was left alone crying out "My Father, My Father! The chariots of Israel and its horsemen." Elisha is left alone, staring up into the sky.

It is readily apparent that the lesson to be learned from this most dramatic scene is that for a great ministry to survive the retirement or leaving of a great leader, there needs to be a plan of succession. The absence of a plan will guarantee a downward spiral of diminishment.

Leaders and their board members need to plan in advance for position changes with precise planning. Jesus trained twelve men to carry the gospel to the ends of the then inhabited world. If that plan had not been in place, Christianity today would only be a chapter or a paragraph in a history book. Instead, it lives all around us.

Each person reading this meditation, needs to prepare for their own "chariot ride". In addition, are you letting others know about the upcoming chariot ride?

Prayer:
"Swing low sweet chariot, coming for to carry me home".
Amen

CREATE

In the beginning, God created the heavens and the earth.
Genesis 1:1
By faith we understand that the universe was created by the word of God, so that what is seen was not made out of things that are visible.
Hebrews 11:3
Remember also your Creator in the days of your youth, before the evil days come and the years draw near of which you will say, "I have no pleasure in them".
Ecclesiastes 12:1

Create is a word that has multiple definitions. Webster's dictionary defines create as the way to come into being by applying imagination. The excellent catechism teacher of my youth, the late Rev. Henry Radius, explained that to create is to make something out of nothing.

The first verse in the Bible states that in the beginning, God created the heavens and the earth. Plainly put, God spoke and literally commanded creation to take place.

Regardless of what you believe regarding how long it took for creation to take place, the one factor which remains is that in the beginning everything all got started with God, the Creator.

A new creation on a different level takes place as a new convert comes to become a follower of Jesus. Such a process is described as becoming a new creation.

[17] Therefore, if anyone is in Christ, he is a new creation.[a] The old has passed away; behold, the new has come. [18] All this is from God, who through Christ reconciled us to himself and gave us the ministry of reconciliation; [19] that is, in Christ God was reconciling[b] the world to himself, not counting their trespasses against them, and entrusting to us the message of reconciliation.
II Corinthians 5:17-19

The death of Christ and his resurrection from the dead formed the beginning of Christ followers being called a new creation. Through Christ's sacrifice all those who followed Christ became a new creation. When we become a new creation, we become a part of human existence that has its roots in Christ and will grow and mature toward a new creation of a new heaven and a new earth.

It is then incumbent on us to join with the writer of Ecclesiastes and to remember our creator from the days of our youth.

What a great creation, all created and designed by God! In this resides man, a fallen creation who by coming to Jesus becomes a new creation! As a new creation, we look ahead to our perfected eternity. There you have it. Are you a part of being a new creation?

Prayer: Psalm 51: 10-11
Father, create in me a clean heart, O God, and renew a right spirit within me. Cast me not away from your presence and take not your Holy Spirit from me. Amen

CREATION

The heavens declare the glory of God,
and the sky above[a] proclaims his handiwork.
² Day to day pours out speech,
and night to night reveals knowledge.
³ There is no speech, nor are there words,
whose voice is not heard.
⁴ Their voice[b] goes out through all the earth,
and their words to the end of the world.
In them he has set a tent for the sun,
⁵   which comes out like a bridegroom leaving his
chamber,
and, like a strong man, runs its course with joy.
⁶ Its rising is from the end of the heavens,
and its circuit to the end of them,
and there is nothing hidden from its heat.
Psalm 19:1-6

A Canadian fishing trip with five other Christian men sounded like excellent therapy to me. I was invited to attend in the absence of one of the regular guys who had to drop out to attend to some problems at his home. I welcomed the change of venue and pace. Mentally I was ready in that my wife of 54 years had gone on to glory the previous year.

The trip was planned with excellence right down to the last detail. Each person was given an assignment on what to bring including being prepared to share a devotional following the evening meal. Psalm 19 seemed perfect to me as a topic to share in this picturesque environment of woods and pristine lake.

Finally, toward the end of the week, I shared my thoughts on "Creation – God's Wordless Book". The meditation was met with questioning of the facts shared. What I had envisioned as being a time of praise evolved into a "raining on the parade" of God's matchless beauty.

A lesson learned from the trip was to be more selective in my fishing companions and to face difficult challenges with a heart of grace rather than my state of internal judgment of the situation.

The most important lesson that I learned was not to expect positive input from all listeners. After all, perhaps maybe they were facing greater problems at home or in their workplace.

Creation is not applauded by all. Many take it as a given that has just evolved many eons ago. In fact when you take God out of creation, you have also dismissed the creator. Going further you are also eliminating the Savior.

Now I feel better, I've unloaded my angst about a fishing trip. However, God remains unchanged. He is the creator. He is the Savior of those who have given their hearts to Him. The question is where are you as you ponder Psalm 19 and consider the glory of God, and the sky above declaring his handiwork? Can you feel the majesty? Can you anticipate the eternity you will have if you follow Jesus for the rest of your life?

Prayer:
Lord let the words of my mouth and the meditation of my heart be acceptable in your sight O Lord, my rock and my redeemer. Amen

DIVISION

[10] According to the grace of God given to me, like a skilled[a] master builder I laid a foundation, and someone else is building upon it. Let each one take care how he builds upon it. [11] For no one can lay a foundation other than that which is laid, which is Jesus Christ. [12] Now if anyone builds on the foundation with gold, silver, precious stones, wood, hay, straw— [13] each one's work will become manifest, for the Day will disclose it, because it will be revealed by fire, and the fire will test what sort of work each one has done. [14] If the work that anyone has built on the foundation survives, he will receive a reward. [15] If anyone's work is burned up, he will suffer loss, though he himself will be saved, but only as through fire. [16] Do you not know that you[b] are God's temple and that God's Spirit dwells in you? [17] If anyone destroys God's temple, God will destroy him. For God's temple is holy, and you are that temple.

I Corinthians 3:10 -17

In the past twenty or so years, mainline Protestant churches have been in turmoil over some key issues that have been clearly explained in scripture as being immoral and sinful.

The issues that are most often debated are homosexuality, gay marriage, transgender, gay church leadership etc. The Bible is very clear that these issues are sinful and therefore abhorrent to a holy God. Also included is the LBGTQ organization which flaunts outright deviation from normal sexual thought and actions.

The topics that divide the mainline denominations have been studied and debated ad nauseum. Churches are breaking denominational ties over these topics.

Part of the splits are between traditional thought and the more modern thought of anything is acceptable. With tongue in cheek thinking, "how could a loving God find loving relationships sinful"?

However, the "elephant in the room" is not depraved sexuality but it really is questioning the absolute authority of the Bible. If the Bible is not the source of absolute truth, then anything goes, and mankind will continue to do what is right in their own eyes.

Revelation 22:18-19 has the last word in this discussion.

[18] I warn everyone who hears the words of the prophecy of this book: if anyone adds to them, God will add to him the plagues described in this book, [19] and if anyone takes away from the words of the book of this prophecy, God will take away his share in the tree of life and in the holy city, which are described in this book.

Prayer:
Holy Father, we tremble at the truth of the message found in Holy Scripture. Forgive us if we have attempted to modify your Word to fit our depraved thinking. We know that your Word is absolute truth. Help us to live in obedience to your Word. In the holy name of Jesus, Amen

DOORS

⁹ I am the door. If anyone enters by me, he will be saved and will go in and out and find pasture.
John10:9

³ At the same time, pray also for us, that God may open to us a door for the word, to declare the mystery of Christ, on account of which I am in prison—
Colossians 4:3

Our lives are surrounded by doors. Doors are utilized for entry and also to close ourselves out from others or to open ourselves to others. Usually, we can control the doors of our lives whether they be the doors of our dwellings or the doors of our private offices.

Each one of us has a door that is open or closed to the hearing of advice and commandments found in the Bible. To those of you who have an open door to your heart for the gospel of Jesus Christ, continue to read because there is definitely an opening on the team for those wishing to share their knowledge and faith in that plan of salvation. You are in a mission field of friends or acquaintances that have placed ajar or closed doors of their hearts to the gospel.

After spending a few years in the education area of school age children and teenagers, the most difficult hurdle to overcome was time! Every time an assignment was issued it always had a deadline attached to the instructions for completion. Invariably, the assignments were completed by the students just prior to the deadline time. However, it was common that a few (normally the same few) came to me with creative reasons as to why they needed more time to hand in their assignment. Other students were very predictable in that their assignments were always on time.

When considering those who have the doors of their hearts ajar or closed to the truth of the gospel, time becomes a critical factor. Their rationale might be putting off coming to Jesus on their own time schedule. However, not one of us knows what the deadline might be. It might be God's plan to shorten our life through death or the second coming of Jesus.

[20] Behold, I stand at the door and knock. If anyone hears my voice and opens the door, I will come in to him and eat with him, and he with me.
Revelation 3:20

Jesus is standing at the door of each person's heart awaiting their response. What's your response? It's a matter of eternal life or death.

Prayer:
Father make me more aware of the eternal importance of my decision to follow your plan of salvation. In the name of Jesus, Amen

EQUIPPED

*[11] And he gave the apostles, the prophets,
the evangelists, the shepherds[a] and teachers,[b] [12] to
equip the saints for the work of ministry, for building
up the body of Christ,*
Ephesians 4:11-12

Henry Aaron of home run fame died in January 2021. The media was buzzing with the tremendous accomplishments of this black athlete. Hank played in his youth with sticks as bats and whatever he could find that could be a ball. The family had almost zero money to spend on sporting equipment. In spite of these odds, Hank made it to the majors. Not only did he make it but he eclipsed Babe Ruth's record for home runs. Most successful batters have seasons that come and go but not "Hammering Hank" who averaged 38 home runs per season and carried a lifetime batting average that exceeded 350. A noted pitcher who played against Hank, said that getting a pitch by Aaron was like "trying to sneak a sunrise past a rooster."

Henry Aaron was a natural athlete. His gifts were God given. Moses was trained in the solitude in the land of Midian to gain his focus. God spoke to him from the midst of a burning bush and called him to lead the exodus. During Moses 40 years in Midian, he gained the concentration that was necessary to lead the grumbling Jews on a 40-year trek.

Jesus' disciples had no formal training other that the business of fishing. As one who has spent much time fishing for recreation, it truly is a sport of solitude and focus. This asset of having a singular goal and sticking to it is a feature that the fishermen exhibited to the point that they changed from fishing for fish to fishing for men. They started Christianity!

One can go on and on and list the many people that were called by God to do specific tasks because they were equipped. Some folks that were unusual but effective in their roles were Sampson, Rahab, Abraham and many others.

Each one of us is gifted. As you think back on your life's experiences, education and present state are you equipped to serve? If so are you active or just observing others that maybe could use your time and or money to build the kingdom through equipping others?

Prayer:
Father, as I sit and think about what I've got in gifts. Please use me at your will, for your service. Amen

EXODUS, AN OASIS

²² Then Moses made Israel set out from the Red Sea, and they went into the wilderness of Shur. They went three days in the wilderness and found no water. ²³ When they came to Marah, they could not drink the water of Marah because it was bitter; therefore it was named Marah. ²⁴ And the people grumbled against Moses, saying, "What shall we drink?" ²⁵ And he cried to the LORD, and the LORD showed him a log, and he threw it into the water, and the water became sweet. There the LORD made for them a statute and a rule, and there he tested them, ²⁶ saying, "If you will diligently listen to the voice of the LORD your God, and do that which is right in his eyes, and give ear to his commandments and keep all his statutes, I will put none of the diseases on you that I put on the Egyptians, for I am the LORD, your healer." ²⁷ Then they came to Elim, where there were twelve springs of water and seventy palm trees, and they encamped there by the water.
Exodus 15:22-27

Whenever I used to think of the Exodus, I was reminded of a bunch of surly grumbling people. My analysis has changed over recent years in that when I read of all the hardships they endured over a forty-year trek, I blush with shame. In my world of adequate food and a choice of an endless variety at my local market, fresh water out of the tap, televisions in multiple rooms, computers for each member of the family and cell phones on an as needed amount etc. Yes, I was so wrong in my critical analysis of the Jews traveling through a desert, going many days without adequate food, water and no shade.

In the early part of the Exodus, they had crossed the Red Sea which God had prepared for them by backing up the water and thus creating a dry route to pass between waters held back by the best dam ever constructed, the mighty hand of God. Their first stop is Marah and they are parched after going three days without fresh water. Marah has water but it's bitter. The people get very vocal with Moses. Moses asks God's help and He advised Moses to throw a nearby log into the bitter water and "voila" it becomes sweet. Problem solved, temporarily.

Before the journey continues, God promises his chosen people that He would give them immunity from all of the plagues and diseases that the Egyptians experienced as a part of the plagues that led to their release from the bondage of slavery imposed by the Egyptians.

The journey continues through the blistering heat and waterless trail. Yes, they could have taken a shorter route to the Promised Land but God led them through a longer route which took about forty years. They had no maps or GPS available but instead followed a cloud by day and an evening fire to show them the way. God was protecting them from checkpoints the Egyptians had established along the shorter route which they had established to get their slave labor back.

The next stop is an oasis. The oasis is called Elim. It's like a spa. It had 12 pools of cool sweet water, enough for one pool per tribe. In addition, there were 70 palm trees offering them shade and probably big ripe juicy dates.

As we travel through our own personal journeys of life, we too are on an exodus that if we are followers of Jesus Christ and believe in the plan of salvation made possible by His death on the cross and His victory over death by His resurrection, we too are bound for the promise of eternity in heaven, a veritable promised land.

Back to Elim. When my grandson named his newborn son Elim, I was not familiar with the desert oasis called Elim. However, after reading today's scripture, the name fits. You see, Elim's mom and dad are Christians. Their wish for their son is that, in this world of challenging exodus paths, he would look to God to be the provider of the oasis of spiritual love and care, and that he would be encouraged to offer the same love and care to others.

As the great grandpa of Elim, it is my daily prayer that he will grow up to represent his name in a most positive manner. So where are you as a reader of this short meditation? Are you perhaps faced with a Marah of bitter water or are you in the shade of a Christ filled oasis that sounds like an Elim resting place on your exodus toward the eternal holy land?

Prayer:
I'm praying the second verse of:
"Guide Me, O Thou Great Jehovah"
Open now the crystal fountain, whence the healing stream doth flow; let the fire and cloudy pillar Lead me all my journey through. Strong Deliverer, strong Deliverer, Be thou still my strength and shield, be thou still my strength and shield. Amen

FAMILY

*¹⁴ For this reason I bow my knees before the
Father, ¹⁵ from whom every family in heaven and on
earth is named, ¹⁶ that according to the riches of his
glory he may grant you to be strengthened with power
through his Spirit in your inner being, ¹⁷ so that Christ
may dwell in your hearts through faith—that you,
being rooted and grounded in love, ¹⁸ may have strength
to comprehend with all the saints what is the breadth
and length and height and depth, ¹⁹ and to know the love
of Christ that surpasses knowledge, that you may be
filled with all the fullness of God.*
Ephesians 3:14-19

I'll admit it, I love to watch sports. My absolute favorite is watching Big Ten football and basketball. However, this year's summer Olympics held in Tokyo caused me to watch many events, especially swimming and track and field. My interest comes quite naturally in that in my high school days, swimming was the sport in which I participated. My two sons both were members of cross country and track teams when they attended high school.

What struck me was that many athletes had a support group watching from "back home". These support groups were composed primarily of family and their close friends. The Covid-19 pandemic barred visitor attendance at the Olympic Games so support groups were often shown as part of a virtual audience.

Today families still gather for baptisms, weddings, funerals and reunions. Hopefully, these gatherings will continue because in our current society we seldom have opportunities to connect with our greater families.

The structure of our society has changed. Social needs are being met on social platforms like Facebook, Twitter and Instagram. We used to call on the phone but now texting has replaced a lot of phone time and personal visits.

What's missing is face to face conversations. We're missing conversations when we have eye to eye contact, facial expression and tone of voice which play a very important part in how we are really feeling.

God placed great emphasis on the family. Abraham was selected by God to begin a family which defied numerical definition. Jacob was the father of the patriarchs. There is no reasonable expectation that we will again meet as families at our grandparent's house after church on Sunday. However, we can make a regular concerted attempt to contact them. You will be amazed how much they know about finances, recipes, hugging and true family histories.

We are all members of the family of God. He is always available to listen to our conversations and pleas. As a family member, are you talking to your heavenly Father? You would be amazed what strength and loving are available in God's family.

Prayer:
Father, I'm going to spend more time talking to you about my concerns. I know you'll answer. In Jesus name, Amen

FIRST MISSION

³⁹ Many Samaritans from that town believed in him because of the woman's testimony, "He told me all that I ever did." ⁴⁰ So when the Samaritans came to him, they asked him to stay with them, and he stayed there two days. ⁴¹ And many more believed because of his word. ⁴² They said to the woman, "It is no longer because of what you said that we believe, for we have heard for ourselves, and we know that this is indeed the Savior of the world."
John 4: 39-42

¹⁴ Now when the apostles at Jerusalem heard that Samaria had received the word of God, they sent to them Peter and John, ¹⁵ who came down and prayed for them that they might receive the Holy Spirit, ¹⁶ for he had not yet fallen on any of them, but they had only been baptized in the name of the Lord Jesus. ¹⁷ Then they laid their hands on them and they received the Holy Spirit.
Acts 8:14-17

All Jews avoided travel through Samaria because they believed that to interact with the Samaritans was a defilement to their spiritual life. So it was customary for Jews to take a rather lengthy route instead of using a shorter route by going through Samaria.

It's noon and it is warm. Jesus goes to Jacob's well in Samaria while his disciples go into Sychar to purchase food. This well had very good water because it was extremely deep. Jesus begins a conversation with a Samaritan woman who was also visiting the well. It's possible that this woman was avoiding gossip because of her checkered past so she visited the well in the middle of the day. Jesus asks her to draw some water for him out of the well.

This is my favorite mission story because I'm led to believe that this is the very first mission effort outside of the Jewish domain. The woman after listening to Jesus's explanation that he is the "living water", comes to be a follower of Jesus. Jesus explains to the woman that he has full knowledge of her many past marriages and that she is now unmarried but living with a man.

The next scene takes place in her village. She can't wait to tell everyone that Jesus knew all about her history and offered her the "living water" of salvation. The disciples after Pentecost bring the Holy Spirit to the Samaritans. All of this mission effort could not have happened if Jesus had avoided Samaria like all his Jewish people.

Without a doubt each one of us have "Samaritans" in our lives. They are the people we avoid because they are not of our class and therefore out of our "comfort zone". They just might be our mission field. Are you up to it?

Prayer:
Heavenly Father, I'm thinking of some individuals that I know just slightly. I haven't let them know that I walk with you. Give me the courage to acquaint them with the "living water". Amen

FUNDRAISING

[25] At present, however, I am going to Jerusalem bringing aid to the saints. [26] For Macedonia and Achaia have been pleased to make some contribution for the poor among the saints at Jerusalem. [27] For they were pleased to do it, and indeed they owe it to them. For if the Gentiles have come to share in their spiritual blessings, they ought also to be of service to them in material blessings. [28] When therefore I have completed this and have delivered to them what has been collected,[a] I will leave for Spain by way of you. [29] I know that when I come to you I will come in the fullness of the blessing[b] of Christ.
[30] I appeal to you, brothers, by our Lord Jesus Christ and by the love of the Spirit, to strive together with me in your prayers to God on my behalf, [31] that I may be delivered from the unbelievers in Judea, and that my service for Jerusalem may be acceptable to the saints, [32] so that by God's will I may come to you with joy and be refreshed in your company. [33] May the God of peace be with you all. Amen.
Romans 15:25-33

In today's world, we are asked to donate to many causes. My daily E-Mail and regular mail contains numerous requests for donations. This has become a mental pain to many of us who are being asked to contribute to causes from all over the USA. Many of the requests are from organizations that we have never heard of. It's almost impossible to figure out which requests are valid and which ones are scams.

The Apostle Paul was nearing the twilight years of his ministry. It appears that he had a "bucket list". He is carrying an offering to Jerusalem, the "mother church" of the expanding growth of Christianity. The offering is coming from the Greek churches who are saying thank you for making them aware of the plan of salvation. Paul is delivering the offering before he heads to Rome and Spain. History tells us that he reached Rome but there is no proof that he made it to Spain before he was executed.

As an aside, the offering from the Greek churches was a thanks offering but in addition it could have included a special thank you to the home of Christianity which were the Jewish people. One wonders why God chose the Jewish people to be the home of the Savior of the World. Could it be that the Greeks who were people that were the home of much philosophical thinking were not just thanking the Jewish church but were looking at the history of the Jewish nation complete with their exodus, Passover and cohesive nature. It is logical to conclude that this offering was a very special offering which was saying thanks to the Jewish church but also to the God that was the creator, sustainer, and author of their salvation.

Back to fundraising. In today's world we support our personal church. How do we fund the many other requests that cross our screens and mailboxes? The easiest thing to do is to ignore all requests unless we know about them. However, we are all responsible stewards of what God has entrusted to our care, custody and control. It is incumbent upon us to do our homework and come to logical conclusions as to how to say "thank you" for God's wonderful plan of salvation. Are you living a thanks filled life? Do your giving patterns reflect a thankful life?

Prayer:
Father accept my thanks for your salvation. Forgive my times of not showing it in giving and in living patterns. In Jesus name, Amen

GRANDMA'S PSALM

I lift up my eyes to the hills.
From where does my help come?
² My help comes from the LORD,
who made heaven and earth.
³ He will not let your foot be moved;
he who keeps you will not slumber.
⁴ Behold, he who keeps Israel
will neither slumber nor sleep.
⁵ The LORD is your keeper;
the LORD is your shade on your right hand.
⁶ The sun shall not strike you by day,
nor the moon by night.
⁷ The LORD will keep you from all evil;
he will keep your life.
⁸ The LORD will keep
your going out and you're coming in
from this time forth and forevermore.
Psalm 121

Sometimes this psalm is called the Soldier's Psalm. Another name for it is the Traveler's Psalm. However, for today's purpose, I'm calling it Grandma's Psalm. Our family tradition was to gather at Grandma's for an annual Christmas celebration. We all looked forward to the gathering. Grandma always had a special dumpling gravy that drew great applause. Another aunt from the Deep South brought a crusty creamed corn dish. However, the menu was usually potluck and quite often there were too many desserts. Naturally, this was a distinct gastronomic delight for us of the younger set.

We ended our gathering with Grandma reading Psalm 121. It was her way of blessing those that she wouldn't see for perhaps another year. She was by definition a saint in her walk with the Lord.

Our eyes look up to the hills for their stoic reminder of strength and permanence. However, our help comes from the Lord who is the creator of heaven and earth. God is always awake and sustaining us which is a miracle that can't be explained but can be worshipped. God has our backs, and he will always sustain us. Just read this psalm when you are at a low point either physically or mentally. In addition, God is always there to help us through the times we are tempted.

So take comfort, whether it be day or night, God is there for you. Not only does God care for us here but he will also care for us eternally. Pass all these words of comfort to your family and rest assured that they are blessed.

Prayer:
Father, thank you for your constant care and love. We need you 24/7. Forgive us when we pat ourselves on the back when in reality, we know our blessings are all from you. Amen

LULLED TO SLEEP

[18] But someone will say, "You have faith and I have works." Show me your faith apart from your works, and I will show you my faith by my works. [19] You believe that God is one; you do well. Even the demons believe—and shudder! [20] Do you want to be shown, you foolish person, that faith apart from works is useless? [21] Was not Abraham our father justified by works when he offered up his son Isaac on the altar? [22] You see that faith was active along with his works, and faith was completed by his works; [23] and the Scripture was fulfilled that says, "Abraham believed God, and it was counted to him as righteousness"—and he was called a friend of God. [24] You see that a person is justified by works and not by faith alone. [25] And in the same way was not also Rahab the prostitute justified by works when she received the messengers and sent them out by another way? [26] For as the body apart from the spirit is dead, so also faith apart from works is dead.
James 2:18-26

James, the half-brother of Jesus is probably the author of the letter of James. James is directly aiming his letter to Christians who are of Jewish origin. They are more than likely house church Christians because the twelve tribes have been scattered. There is a great deal of apathy in the hearts and lives of these Jewish Christians. One can truly assess their behavior as "doing what was right in their own eyes." This same type of mindset was used to describe the Jewish people between the leadership of the judges and just before the kings took over.

There are many similarities with the recipients of James' letter and our society of today. American behavior of today has strayed to also truly doing what is "right in our own eyes". It has happened gradually and we haven't really responded to the changes that have gradually taken over. Our family structure has splintered, and we are so consumed with two parents working outside the home and busy school schedules that we really don't have quality time together. Our sexual mores have drastically changed. Gender is decided by youth as early as elementary school. Marriage is rapidly being replaced by meaningful relationships. Some of which are only for the pleasure of one night. During our waning Covid-19 pandemic, when America spent a great deal of time at home, Bible reading dropped from 13-9%. Drinking, drugs and in home movies increased. Also, suicides increased. Truly America is doing "what is right in our own eyes."

Where is the outrage? We have been lulled to sleep. We are like an idling car that is not put into gear and driven. We are similar to beautiful yachts that are not put to sea and only spend time tied to their dock space.

It is at a time such as this that the church needs to take leadership. They have the Word. It is "watered down" in many pulpits. The "Comfortable Pew" was the title of a book that grabbed great popularity some years ago. The name is quite accurate.

So where are you in assessing your wakefulness during this time of spiritual and moral decline? Are you too comfortable to say, "Enough is enough"?

Prayer:

Father, forgive our sins of moral apathy. Our church attendance is not enough. We can make a difference. Give us the courage to speak up for you! Amen

MEDITATION

[14] Let the words of my mouth and the meditation of my heart
be acceptable in your sight,
O LORD, my rock and my redeemer.
Psalm 19:14

"What are you doing for your meditations" was a question posed to me by my grandson. What an eye-opening topic! It just so happened that the book I was using for my time of meditation was the same book that my grandson had recently used. Not only were we meshed by a common DNA but also we were "on the same page" in our meditation life. The rest of the dinner was a great renewing of experiences that we had encountered in our many months apart.

The drive home was a time of thinking regarding the role of meditations in the lives of today's church members. Many go to services with great regularity, they give of their finances, they discuss the efficacy of recent sermons but what seems to be missing are stories of what God has done and is doing in their lives. Could it possibly be that something is missing?

Back to meditations. Is it possible that many who regularly attend church and have done so are unable to relate how God has and is working in their lives? Would it not make good sense for those of us who are lifelong church members to take time to have a conversation with their creator, savior and sustainer? We wouldn't miss our annual physical of our physical bodies. How about our spiritual soul?

God knows your heart. He cares for you and wants you to have a rock-solid assurance that you know what your future is after you breathe your last earthly breath.

Talk to God in your meditations and be able to say "I'm yours Lord, everything I've got, everything I'm not -I'm yours. Arms open wide! Amen

MIRACLES, SIGNS, WONDERS AND GIFTS

*2 Therefore we must pay much closer attention to what
we have heard, lest we drift away from it. ² For since the
message declared by angels proved to be reliable,
and every transgression or disobedience received a
just retribution, ³ how shall we escape if we neglect such
a great salvation? It was declared at first by the Lord,
and it was attested to us by those who heard, ⁴ while
God also bore witness by signs and wonders and
various miracles and by gifts of the Holy
Spirit distributed according to his will.
Hebrews 2: 1-4*

If I were in a classroom that was devoted to the
discussion of miracles, I might begin one day by asking
those present if they had witnessed any miracles in their
lives. I suspect that the response would be close to none.
Could it be that today's sophisticated world of scientific
achievement would be the answer to events of cures and
healings and would be explained to have their basis found
in medications and/or medical procedures? However,
there are scientific breakthroughs especially in the areas
of vaccines and new drugs that are so effective that
viruses and other diseases can be totally arrested by
man's ingenuity. As a society, we can solve most of our
medical problems by laboratory products, we really don't
wait for or recognize miracles when they occur.

This past week a family member experienced a medical miracle. She is a young mother and Christian schoolteacher that has always been in the best of health. One day she experienced what appeared to be a small symptom and after explaining the problem to her husband who is a registered nurse at the main Mayo Clinic said that it should be checked. The diagnosis was a form of sarcoma which was very rare and healing was not really expected. However, an experimental drug was utilized, and the cancer was stabilized. The young mom felt great all through the treatment and continued her regular roles of motherhood and teacher. A miracle in the making?

However, a CAT scan bought devastating news. Two new tumors and no known correlation to the sarcoma. The oncologist had a difficult role to map out a treatment and it took about a month before he sat down with the husband and wife to discuss future therapy. He came into the consultation room and exclaimed "I just don't understand it but your latest CAT scan is clear. There are no tumors!"

Back to the classroom. "Class what you just heard is a miracle." Jesus utilized miracles to add emphasis to his teaching. When you witness a miracle, it is your job to call it a miracle and then to give credit to the Great Physician.

We do have miracles today. We as Christians have been slow to acknowledge the existence of a miracle when we encounter one. We need to be aware of our surroundings. When we observe the signs in our lives and in those of our friends, there are many signs, wonders and miracles. If we don't give God the credit for his work in our lives, then who will?

Prayer:

Give me increased awareness of your signs, wonders and miracles. When I observe them and am nudged by the Holy Spirit give me the situations that I can point others to you. Amen

NOAH FOUND FAVOR

When man began to multiply on the face of the land and daughters were born to them, ² the sons of God saw that the daughters of man were attractive. And they took as their wives any they chose. ³ Then the LORD said, "My Spirit shall not abide in man forever, for he is flesh: his days shall be 120 years." ⁴ The Nephilim were on the earth in those days, and also afterward, when the sons of God came into the daughters of man and they bore children to them. These were the mighty men who were of old, the men of renown.
⁵ The LORD saw that the wickedness of man was great in the earth, and that every intention of the thoughts of his heart was only evil
continually. ⁶ And the LORD regretted that he had made man on the earth, and it grieved him to his heart.
Genesis 6:1-6

Noah found favor in the eyes of the Lord. God designated Noah and his family of eight to be saved from the upcoming flood.

By faith, Noah being warned by God concerning events as yet unseen, in reverent fear constructed an ark for the saving of his household. By this he condemned the world and became an heir of the righteousness that comes by faith.
Hebrews 11:7

Since the catastrophic flood, there has never been so complete a devastation of the earth and its inhabitants. We do know that the world will be subject to total change when Jesus comes again at the second resurrection.

Assuming that you are a follower of Jesus, do you think God has a mandate for us? It is obvious that sin is rampant, and the world is basically a very evil environment. When Jesus was in the process of ascending, He issued the **Great Commission.** *But you will receive power when the Holy Spirit has come upon you, and you will be my witnesses in Jerusalem and in all Judea and Samaria, and to the end of the earth. Acts 1:8*

So how do we implement those parting words of Jesus? Based upon our analysis of the great sinful nature of the earth, is it time for us to "hunker down" like Noah and save only our families? The real question is how are we responsible for helping implement the Great Commission?

For a no-nonsense answer to the question, did Noah attempt to spread the gospel to his peers? To ask the question, is to answer it. Just imagine the conversations that observers must have had while observing Noah building the ark. Bear in mind that the ark was 75' wide x 45' high x 450' long. Just imagine the questions:

1. There's going to be a flood? We're living in the desert.
2. What's your plan to round up the animals?
3. Why would God send a flood? We're enjoying life and minding our own business?
4. Pretty cruel, saving animals and drowning all the people.
5. Have you really thought this over?

Noah certainly had conversations with those that saw his construction project. So how can we spread the gospel? The answer is simple. We can talk to others, we can contribute to Christian causes that are spreading the gospel, we can support our local church etc.

Prayer:
    Father, may I find favor in your eyes. Amen

OPINION

⁷ For none of us lives to himself, and none of us dies to himself. ⁸ For if we live, we live to the Lord, and if we die, we die to the Lord. So then, whether we live or whether we die, we are the Lord's. ⁹ For to this end Christ died and lived again, that he might be Lord both of the dead and of the living.
¹⁰ Why do you pass judgment on your brother? Or you, why do you despise your brother? For we will all stand before the judgment seat of God; ¹¹ for it is written, "As I live, says the Lord, every knee shall bow to me, and every tongue shall confess to God."
¹² So then each of us will give an account of himself to God.
Romans 14:7-12

Weak Christians are those that obey the details of the law. Perhaps those who enjoy their freedom in Christ are more mature in their Christian walk.

St. Augustine gave fine guidance to us in how to live and how to accept others "In essentials, unity, in non-essentials, liberty, in all things, charity."

Being correct in our demeanor is essential. We as followers of Jesus should do everything to honor Christ in our personal walk. In our attempts to follow Christ are we "keeping score" of how others live and use their lives to assess our own loyalty in following Christ?

It is necessary to follow the rules of golf when playing in competition. One is expected to be honest and accurate in personal score keeping without moving the ball for a better lie or taking a penalty stroke when expected. In fact, serious golfers shy away from players that cheat and 'fudge" when they play.

We need to be totally honest when we assess our own personal walk with God. Comparing ourselves to others is not how God judges our walk. He knows our actions and our words, and He knows our hearts. There is no room for falseness. Yes, God has forgiven our sins. However true Christians make every attempt to avoid sin and to live a God honoring life. We need to count every stroke, not improve our lie and "gimmees" are not allowed. So how's your walk?

Prayer:
Father accept my personal life. Forgive my sins including the ones that I have overlooked by comparing myself to others. An old hymn comes to mind:

Living for Jesus a life that is true,
Striving to please Him in all that I do;
Yielding allegiance, glad hearted and free,
This is the pathway of blessing for me.

In Jesus holy name, Amen

PARTIALITY

*My brothers, show no partiality as you hold the faith in
our Lord Jesus Christ, the Lord of glory. ² For if a man
wearing a gold ring and fine clothing comes into your
assembly, and a poor man in shabby clothing also
comes in, ³ and if you pay attention to the one who
wears the fine clothing and say, "You sit here in a good
place," while you say to the poor man, "You stand over
there," or, "Sit down at my feet," ⁴ have you not then
made distinctions among yourselves and become judges
with evil thoughts? ⁵ Listen, my beloved brothers, has
not God chosen those who are poor in the world to
be rich in faith and heirs of the kingdom, which he has
promised to those who love him? ⁶ But you have
dishonored the poor man. Are not the rich the ones who
oppress you, and the ones who drag you into
court? ⁷ Are they not the ones who blaspheme the
honorable name by which you were called?*
James 2:1-7

Partiality was not a part of my thinking when I was
in my earlier years. The friends that I enjoyed were from
an assortment of financial backgrounds ranging from
parents who were quite wealthy to those who were living
from paycheck to paycheck. Social status was not part of
my thinking until I started dating Susan. Upon one
occasion Susan's mother requested that I park my modest
older Plymouth offsite because it didn't fit with the autos
soon to arrive carrying the guests of their late afternoon
gala. Needless to say, Susan and I became very platonic
in our friendship level from that day forward. I believe
that Rosa Parks and I shared a similar feeling when she
experienced partiality in where she was expected to sit on
a urban bus. The feeling was truly gut wrenching.

Now that I have lived beyond the biblical expectation of threescore and ten, my thinking regarding partiality has remained but has grown into a more mature assessment. As a society, we arrange ourselves by outward appearance. Certain invitations range from black tie to business casual expectations. As a side note "Sunday Best" has morphed into "business casual" in many church worship settings. Probably an effective guideline as to what to wear to church is what will your guests wear whom you invite to worship with you.

The elite leaders in the Old Testament had a dress code that was mandated by God. However, we have non biblical based knowledge of how worshippers dressed when they attended the synagogue. Jesus and his disciples didn't wear special clothes when they taught their followers.

Proper wedding attire was expected during New Testament times. In fact, Jesus used the illustration of a wedding feast in one of his parables where proper wedding attire was expected (John 22).

Making assessments about exterior dress needs to be changed. God looks at the heart of a person. We need to do the same especially when we talk to someone about Jesus.

When someone visits our church, we need to be warm and friendly. It just might be someone who is looking for Jesus because the Spirit is at work within their heart.

Prayer:

Heavenly Father, give me a heart that looks at others who are also made in your image that we encounter in life. May my conversation be one that reveals my being one of your children that is very interested in leading others to you? In Jesus name, Amen

PERSISTENCE

And he told them a parable to the effect that they
ought always to pray and not lose heart. ² He said, "In a
certain city there was a judge who neither feared God
nor respected man. ³ And there was a widow in that city
who kept coming to him and saying, 'Give me justice
against my adversary.' ⁴ For a while he refused, but
afterward he said to himself, 'Though I neither fear God
nor respect man, ⁵ yet because this widow keeps
bothering me, I will give her justice, so that she will not
beat me down by her continual coming.'" ⁶ And the
Lord said, "Hear what the unrighteous judge
says. ⁷ And will not God give justice to his elect, who cry
to him day and night? Will he delay long over them? ⁸ I
tell you, he will give justice to them speedily.
Nevertheless, when the Son of Man comes, will he find
faith on earth?"
Luke 18:1-8

Jesus is teaching on the importance of continual
prayer. Luke is the author of the above scripture, and he
reports in his writings of Jesus' illustration of a widow's
plight. Luke was a physician by education and practice.
His heart for others was a source of motivation to write
about the aspects of Jesus' ministry that involved people
in need such as widows and those in need of healing.

A judge in Luke's time was basically a circuit
judge that operated out of a tent that he moved from
location to location based upon needs in the vicinity.
People wishing to gain audience with the judge paid a fee
or bribe. Women never were given an interview with the
judge unless accompanied by a man. However, the

widow in today's scripture was persistent. She kept "hounding" the judge until he finally gave in just to make her "go away".

How do we get heard when we pray? Our Father in heaven is always available. We don't have to pay a bribe or a fee to approach God. We don't need to pray through anyone else. Our prayers are direct. We have direct access.

The widow's persistence teaches us to be continual in our prayers. This means that prayer should be a primary option to seek help in whatever areas that troubles us. I inwardly cringe when I hear fellow Christians exclaiming" I guess all that we can do now is pray" This is typically said when there seems to be no earthly solution that is available. "Give me a break". Prayer should be our first and ongoing avenue of seeking help.

There you have it. God will listen to your every prayer whether it be of thought or verbal. He' waiting to talk to your soul. He's listening. Are you praying?

Prayer:
Lord listen to your children praying,
Lord send your Spirit in this place
Lord listen to your children praying
Send us love, send us power, send us grace!
    Amen

PETER

³ Blessed be the God and Father of our Lord Jesus Christ! According to his great mercy, he has caused us to be born again to a living hope through the resurrection of Jesus Christ from the dead, ⁴ to an inheritance that is imperishable, undefiled, and unfading, kept in heaven for you, ⁵ who by God's power are being guarded through faith for a salvation ready to be revealed in the last time. ⁶ In this you rejoice, though now for a little while, if necessary, you have been grieved by various trials, ⁷ so that the tested genuineness of your faith—more precious than gold that perishes though it is tested by fire—may be found to result in praise and glory and honor at the revelation of Jesus Christ. ⁸ Though you have not seen him, you love him. Though you do not now see him, you believe in him and rejoice with joy that is inexpressible and filled with glory, ⁹ obtaining the outcome of your faith, the salvation of your souls.
I Peter 1:3-9

In today's scripture, the apostle Peter is writing to Christians, mostly Gentiles, in the Roman Provinces of Asia Minor north of the Taurus Mountain range which today is known as Turkey. Peter has been a Christian for about 30 years and is nearing the end of his ministry. Now he takes time to write what's on his heart. In about 4-5 years he will die as a martyr.

Peter fascinates me. He has lived his life "on the edge". His impulsive nature shines through in his walking on the water toward Jesus, his absolute denial of Jesus just prior to the crucifixion and finally his walk with Jesus shortly after the resurrection. In that walk, Jesus very pointedly asks Peter "do you love me" three times. Each time Peter responds with a version of *"Yes Lord, you know that I love you". Jesus responds each time by telling Peter "feed my sheep".* Peter is now commissioned by Jesus to begin his 30 plus year ministry of feeding Jesus' sheep. (Recorded in John 21:15-19)

Many of us can possibly identify with Peter. I'm certainly one of them. As I look back on my life, there have been conversations and actions that have taken place. Our personal histories can't be changed but they can be forgiven completely by the plan of salvation made possible by the death and resurrection of Jesus.

Are you perhaps in the same crowd that I'm in, "guilty but forgiven"? If you are, then pause and thank God for his plan of salvation.

If, however you have doubts, then read what Peter has to say through his words found in 1 Peter 1:3-9. This might just be the opportunity to have a talk with Jesus like Peter had after Jesus' resurrection.

Prayer:
Father, I need to have a talk with you as Peter did just before his ministry started. Mold my desires to show others that you live within my life for now and for all eternity. In Jesus name, Amen

PRAYER BEYOND WORDS

26 Likewise the Spirit helps us in our weakness. For we do not know what to pray for as we ought, but the Spirit himself intercedes for us with groanings too deep for words. 27 And he who searches hearts knows what is the mind of the Spirit because the Spirit intercedes for the saints according to the will of God.
Romans 8:26-27

We often refer to prayer in a somewhat casual manner. When someone is being overcome by an illness that appears to be incurable by the use of human medicine, we often hear someone say "well it appears that all we have left is prayer". Really? Prayers need to be the first and continual approach to all of our needs. God has surrounded us with very effective medicine. However, they are a part of God's master plan for our lives. In no way are they our only way of seeking answers to the problems that we face.

When things are going your way and life is very positive, how's your prayer life? Mine is not as intentional and fervent when things are going my way. It is quite obvious that we don't grow in our faith unless we are faced with concerns and/or problems. It is especially at this point that the Holy Spirit takes our prayers and clarifies them to our Heavenly Father with groanings and language beyond our comprehension.

Note that the Holy Spirit prays on our behalf with groanings and words too deep for us to understand. The Spirit knows the Father's will and consequently those prayers will all be answered. Sometimes those answers are not to our liking, but they will be answered.

61

The preceding scripture gives me great comfort. It tells me that regardless of how poorly my prayers are worded that the Holy Spirit will clarify my prayers to the Father. The Holy Spirit is interceding for us but is not praying when we fail to pray. When we are intentional in our prayers, the Holy Spirit lifts us up to the Father with greater clarity.

So how is your prayer life? Are you intentional or are you sort of praying "off the cuff"? Prayer is so important that you are urged to pray often, pray as you go about your work, and pray as you travel. In fact pray as often as you can. The Spirit will assist you whenever you pray. What a great comfort!

Prayer:
Heavenly Father, thank you for always being available to hear our prayers. We are never put on hold, but you listen whenever we pray. So listen to this prayer and the individual prayers of my family and acquaintances. In Jesus name, Amen

PRIDE

*⁹ He also told this parable to some who trusted in
themselves that they were righteous, and treated others
with contempt: ¹⁰ "Two men went up into the temple to
pray, one a Pharisee and the other a tax collector. ¹¹ The
Pharisee, standing by himself, prayed[a] thus: 'God, I
thank you that I am not like other men, extortioners,
unjust, adulterers, or even like this tax collector. ¹² I fast
twice a week; I give tithes of all that I get.' ¹³ But the tax
collector, standing far off, would not even lift up his
eyes to heaven, but beat his breast, saying, 'God, be
merciful to me, a sinner!' ¹⁴ I tell you, this man went
down to his house justified, rather than the other.
For everyone who exalts himself will be humbled, but
the one who humbles himself will be exalted.
Luke 18:9-14*

Becoming guilty of the sin of pride is so easy to
fall into. When one is praised for a job well done, it is
very easy to slide into the mode of personal thinking that
one truly is that type of excellent person.

Some nonprofits print the names of their
benefactors in categories which indicates their level of
giving. Perhaps pride is the motivating factor that leads
one to give to a prideful amount. The other side of this
equation is that the listing of donors can be an incentive
for others to give more monies to achieve a higher
published bracket. The anonymous giver is a category
that is very interesting and the motivation of for that
category of giving is between that individual and God.
Of course, the motivation for all levels of giving is
always known to God.

There is no right answer to know how to avoid the sin of self-conceit. Perhaps the condition of one's careful analysis of the teachings of the nonprofit is probably a deciding criteria which should be looked at before one donates to the institution. Administrative costs are a key factor.

An illustration of analytic giving is an acquaintance of mine who has since gone on to glory. God had blessed this man with more money than he needed. His friends often asked him why he drove an older car and lived in a rather modest home. His response is that instead of a newer car his monies were supporting individuals to attend seminary to prepare to become pastors but who really couldn't afford it. I happened to meet one of the pastors that had received his tuition gift and he said that if he had not received it, he could never have afforded to attend seminary.

So how does one decide to give? It's between you and God. It's just like the Pharisee and the tax collector, it's a matter of where one's heart is at.

Prayer:
Father, help me to consult you before I send out another check. I need to become humble in my giving. Amen

READY OR NOT

³ As he sat on the Mount of Olives, the disciples came to him privately, saying, "Tell us, when will these things be, and what will be the sign of your coming and of the end of the age?" ⁴ And Jesus answered them, "See that no one leads you astray. ⁵ For many will come in my name, saying, 'I am the Christ,' and they will lead many astray. ⁶ And you will hear of wars and rumors of wars. See that you are not alarmed, for this must take place, but the end is not yet. ⁷ For nation will rise against nation, and kingdom against kingdom, and there will be famines and earthquakes in various places. ⁸ All these are but the beginning of the birth pains.
⁹ "Then they will deliver you up to tribulation and put you to death, and you will be hated by all nations for my name's sake. ¹⁰ And then many will fall away and betray one another and hate one another. ¹¹ And many false prophets will arise and lead many astray. ¹² And because lawlessness will be increased, the love of many will grow cold.
Matthew 24:3-12

Many of us can remember a game called "hide and seek". The seeker would count to a predetermined number and shout "here I come, ready or not".

The above scripture for consideration points out that one day everything as we know it will come to an end. We will have zero advanced warning as to when, but we are told that we need to be aware of many warning signs such as earthquakes, wild weather, nations fighting each other etc. These are signs for us to be prepared for the second coming of Christ when our world as we know it will come to a screeching halt.

Some of you might wonder if Jesus is ever coming back because you see so many signs of the end times. We are not only ravaged by intense hostility between nations but our nation is more polarized politically than ever in its history. Other nations are building atomic arsenals and have developed technology that will lock up our technology rendering us helpless.

We truly are a nation that is doing what is right in our own eyes. Abortion is accepted as the right of a woman to choose the life or death of her in vitro baby. Our politics are dividing families and friendships. Civil discussion of political differences was once a fun topic but now it is too intense to discuss.

So when will Jesus ever come back? Things are beyond our comprehension. II Peter 3:8 says that God's calendar is far different than ours. To Him a thousand years are as one day to us and one day is as a thousand years.

We just don't know when this world will cease to exist. We do know that its end is inevitable. The obvious question is this: are you afraid to face the second coming? Are you prepared by having chosen to follow Jesus? Today is still a day of grace. You can ask for forgiveness of your past, present and future life's sins. Jesus died on the cross so that all the sins of his followers would be forgiven. Today would be a great time for you to give your life over to following Jesus. He's waiting and knocking at the door of your heart. This is a decision that really can't be put off.

Prayer:
Father listen to your children asking for your forgiveness. Give them a peace of knowing that they are yours forever. In Jesus holy name, Amen.

SHEPHERDS

[35] And Jesus went throughout all the cities and villages, teaching in the synagogues and proclaiming the gospel of the kingdom and healing every disease and every affliction. [36] When he saw the crowds, he had compassion for them, because they were harassed and helpless, like sheep without a shepherd. *[37] Then he said to his disciples, "The harvest is plentiful, but the laborers are few; [38] therefore pray earnestly to the Lord of the harvest to send laborers into his harvest."*
Matthew 9: 35-38

All of us are sheep. Jesus is the chief shepherd. We often refer to a pastor as an under shepherd in that his role is to be as a shepherd to the church that he serves.

When Jesus looked out over the crowd of people that were listening to his proclamation of the gospel, Jesus assessed the crowd as sheep that needed a shepherd.

In the Old Testament the shepherds were first the judges, and they were followed by many kings. However, in the New Testament the main shepherds are the elders whose roles are to watch over the flock of sheep within the church. A function of the elders is to equip the church members to be active in ministry. Many of the congregational members are gifted by God to fulfill the role of shepherds.

Shepherds in the Old Testament times tended sheep 24/7. This was especially important at night because then animal predators were quite often attempting to snatch sheep out of the fold. The shepherds worked in teams because the gate of the fold had to be protected all night. When daybreak came the sheep knew the voice of their particular shepherd and they would follow his lead because they recognized his voice.

As church members we all have an assortment of gifts, and many members of the congregation are gifted in the area of shepherding. If you are exercising your role of shepherding, the sheep within your area of influence recognize and respect your voice and they will follow your leading. Are you exercising that role of shepherding? The church of today needs strong leadership of the sheep. Are you up to it?

Prayer:
Heavenly Father give us hearts that have a sensitivity for the sheep within our area of influence and may we lead them to be a stronger flock for your kingdom. Amen

SOURDOUGH

[36] "But concerning that day and hour no one knows, not even the angels of heaven, nor the Son, but the Father only. [37] For as were the days of Noah, so will be the coming of the Son of Man. [38] For as in those days before the flood they were eating and drinking, marrying, and giving in marriage, until the day when Noah entered the ark, [39] and they were unaware until the flood came and swept them all away, so will be the coming of the Son of Man.
Matthew 24:36-39

Sourdough was a label which was tacked on to some of the early settlers of Alaska or Northwest Canada. These early pioneers were mostly prospecting for gold and they carried in their possessions fermented dough. They used the dough to make bread at sporadic times. The dough was probably similar to the leaven which was used by the Jews at about the time of the exodus.

Leaven is a substance when added to dough produces carbon dioxide and thereby causes the dough to rise and become more porous.

However, the Jews were instructed by God through his servant Moses to be ready for the exodus right after the last plague. They were instructed to be fully dressed to travel immediately, to eat a roasted lamb and not leave any leftovers. They were not to utilize leaven because it would add too much time to their quick beginning of the exodus out of Egypt. A key ingredient in their planning for their pending exodus was to be ready to leave in a moment's notice.

In a similar fashion, we are all on an exodus in that we are going to leave our mortality behind, and leave headed for immortality without being aware of the leaving time in advance.

Not one of us knows when we will breathe our last breath or when Jesus will come at the second resurrection. There will not be enough time to wait for your figurative bread to rise. Are you ready to leave?

Prayer:
Father, only you know when our mortal lives will end. We know we need to always be prepared. Forgive us if we are not ready. Erase our doubts and give us assurance. We are beginning to see the urgency. Soften our hearts to give ourselves to your service. Amen

TEMPLE

^{15} If anyone's work is burned up, he will suffer loss, though he himself will be saved, but only as through fire.
^{16} Do you not know that you are God's temple and that God's Spirit dwells in you? ^{17} If anyone destroys God's temple, God will destroy him. For God's temple is holy, and you are that temple.
^{18} Let no one deceive himself. If anyone among you thinks that he is wise in this age, let him become a fool that he may become wise. ^{19} For the wisdom of this world is folly with God. For it is written, "He catches the wise in their craftiness," ^{20} and again, "The Lord knows the thoughts of the wise, that they are futile."
I Corinthians 3:15-20

It appears that we are living in a time very similar to that of the Jews who were doing was right in their own eyes (Jdg. 17:6b) just after the last judge and before their first king. Today there are very limited standards of morality. It would appear that if an activity is pleasurable and no one gets hurt, it's okay.

Some illustrations attesting to our declining morals are seen in the number of unwed mothers giving birth and not having any idea as to who the father might be. In fact, our national laws do not allow for any form of discrimination in how people are treated regardless of their sexual preference.

Yet in the scripture from Corinthians, we see that sexual expression is in fact a spiritual act. If we become united with someone outside of marriage, we are sinning against what God has demanded of us. When we treat our bodies as temples, we are to take care of it in every way possible. This involves, diet, sleep, exercise, and moral behavior.

Before you pass judgment on this meditation as being old fashioned and out of date, be aware that God has not changed but our society has. Someday, each one of us will be asked how we have treated our personal body temples.

Prayer:
Father, my temple needs my attention. Please give me the moral strength to make the right decisions in its care. Amen

THE COST

[57] As they were going along the road, someone said to him, "I will follow you wherever you go." [58] And Jesus said to him, "Foxes have holes, and birds of the air have nests, but the Son of Man has nowhere to lay his head." [59] To another he said, "Follow me." But he said, "Lord, let me first go and bury my father." [60] And Jesus said to him, "Leave the dead to bury their own dead. But as for you, go and proclaim the kingdom of God." [61] Yet another said, "I will follow you, Lord, but let me first say farewell to those at my home." [62] Jesus said to him, "No one who puts his hand to the plow and looks back is fit for the kingdom of God."
Luke 9:57-62

In our current society, the cost of a purchase or an activity is seriously considered before one completes a transaction.

Jesus is teaching his followers during the initial stages of his earthly ministry what constitutes the true cost of being a Jesus follower. Jesus never interviewed possible future followers multiple times such as is done in today's hiring practices. It is expected that multiple phone interviews will preface an actual face to face interview before an offer to hire is rendered.

An initial response to Jesus' invitation to follow him was expected to be immediate and without personal and/or considerations to be met before one would drop everything and follow Jesus. It almost sounds as if Jesus' offers of calling are unreasonable in that Jesus expected an immediate positive response without any personal reservations. However, when one considers the origin of the call to follow, then it is apparent that Jesus has already prepared the heart of the one being asked and knows that there will be acceptance without existing baggage.

It needs to be recognized that the Holy Spirit works in many hearts of those who are in the process of being called to be followers of our Savior.

The Apostle Paul was prepared by being a Jew of the tribe of Benjamin, trained by Gamaliel to be a Pharisee. In addition, Paul was a registered Roman citizen. Paul was using his unique background to persecute Christians before he met Jesus on the road to Damascus and experienced a most dramatic change of heart and personal calling.

As you look back upon your life, do you see the hand of God preparing you for your role in ministry? You can avoid the question by saying that you haven't been called. Are you a Jesus follower? If so, then you have been called to ministry right where you live and work. Those people that interact with you comprise your personal mission field. So what is the cost? Do your peers know that you walk with the Master? If not, isn't it about time?

Prayer;
Lord of my life and the Master of my today and future, give me the motivation and opportunity to let others know the path that I'm on and then invite others to join. Amen

DAY OF THE LORD

⁴ They will say, "Where is the promise of his coming? For ever since the fathers fell asleep, all things are continuing as they were from the beginning of creation." ⁵ For they deliberately overlook this fact, that the heavens existed long ago, and the earth was formed out of water and through water by the word of God, ⁶ and that by means of these the world that then existed was deluged with water and perished. ⁷ But by the same word the heavens and earth that now exist are stored up for fire, being kept until the Day of Judgment and destruction of the ungodly.

⁸ But do not overlook this one fact, beloved, that with the Lord one day is as a thousand years, and a thousand years as one day. ⁹ The Lord is not slow to fulfill his promise as some count slowness, but is patient toward you, not wishing that any should perish, but that all should reach repentance. ¹⁰ But the day of the Lord will come like a thief, and then the heavens will pass away with a roar, and the heavenly bodies will be burned up and dissolved, and the earth and the works that are done on it will be exposed.

II Peter 3:4-10

The "Day of the Lord" is liberally sprinkled throughout the Bible. For this scripture authored by the Apostle Peter it speaks to the second coming of Jesus or the Second Resurrection.

It is vividly explained as a day that will occur without warning. Our present universe will evaporate with a roar. We know from the scriptures that the Day of the Lord will happen, however no one knows when. Peter is writing these words while incarcerated in a Roman prison about four years before his death. Peter, no doubt knew that his prison stay would probably end in his death. One can just feel the urgency of his God inspired words.

Today, few people are concerned about the end of time as we know it. We do know that our heavenly Father knows that exact time when it will take place. The Father is patient and desires his image bearers to have every opportunity to come to him as followers.

Biblical scholars are divided as to whether the universe will totally be destroyed or that it will be redone into a perfect and sinless state. Many believe that our bodies will be changed to be similar to Jesus' body after the first resurrection. Jesus glorified body would just appear magically without needing to enter a room through a door. We do know that those who have predeceased us will rise and will receive their glorified body that will last for eternity to live with Jesus.

The Day of the Lord is a fact that needs to be dealt with. Can you think of a more pressing topic? Do you know what will happen to you when the Day of the Lord takes place? There can be no more important topic that you will ever face. It truly is of life and death importance.

Here is a simple prayer that will guarantee you're becoming a Jesus follower:
Dear God, I know that I'm a sinner. I want to turn from my sins and ask for your forgiveness. I believe that Jesus Christ is your son. I believe He died for my sins and that you raised Him to life. I want Him to come into my heart and to take control of my life. I want to trust Jesus as my Savior and follow Him as my Lord from this day forward. In Jesus Name, Amen.

THE GREATEST COMMANDMENT

*"Now this is the commandment—the statutes and the
rules that the L*ORD *your God commanded me to teach
you, that you may do them in the land to which you are
going over, to possess it, ² that you may fear
the L*ORD *your God, you and your son and your son's
son, by keeping all his statutes and his commandments,
which I command you, all the days of your life, and that
your days may be long. ³ Hear therefore, O Israel, and
be careful to do them, that it may go well with you, and
that you may multiply greatly, as the L*ORD*, the God of
your fathers, has promised you, in a land flowing with
milk and honey.
⁴ "Hear, O Israel: The L*ORD *our God, the L*ORD *is
one. ⁵ You shall love the L*ORD *your God with all your
heart and with all your soul and with all your
might. ⁶ And these words that I command you today
shall be on your heart. ⁷ You shall teach them diligently
to your children and shall talk of them when you sit in
your house, and when you walk by the way, and when
you lie down, and when you rise. ⁸ You shall bind them
as a sign on your hand, and they shall be as frontlets
between your eyes. ⁹ You shall write them on the
doorposts of your house and on your gates.
Deuteronomy 6: 1-9*

The above scripture is an Israelite mandate for
daily living. It is called the Shema and is the Jewish
confession of faith. It is taught to children as soon as they

learn to speak. It is repeated upon arising and at the end of the day.

By contrast, since the reformation, catechism has been taught in most Christ centered churches. Today that instruction has waned down to almost zero. In addition, public education has restricted God and prayer from their curriculums. Biblical teaching is left to home, church and Christian schools.

Television shows the lack of biblical knowledge. Many game show questions based upon simple Bible questions are seldom answered correctly. "Man on the street" interviews reflect the same lack of biblical knowledge. Similar questions would have been answered correctly by elementary age students with ease in earlier years.

In addition to the lack of biblical knowledge comes the current living pattern of today's society of "doing what is right in our own eyes." It's a natural chain of events which are a part of our cultural downward spiral.

Starting in our institutions of higher learning, absolute truth was relegated as being nonexistent. What was inserted on a gradual basis is that America was founded by racists. The founding of America to escape a mandated state has been deleted from our classrooms. We are being led by educators to believe that if you are Caucasian you are bias and racist.

Then the Covid-19 pandemic hit and parents began to question the textbooks being utilized in public schools and now more and more schools are being questioned as to what they are teaching. Personally, I see the hand of God in the sequence of events that has caused parents to analyze what their children are being taught.

This national dilemma is being slowly fixed by parents who are attending school board meetings and asking questions regarding curriculum content.

Another factor needs to be inserted in that America desperately needs a revival.

They need to realize that Jesus is the singular way to heaven. Churches also need to look at what they are preaching as being the gospel. We as a nation need to return to what our founding fathers believed.

Prayer:
Father look down upon us and give us an inner strength to question those that we have hired to teach our children. Also, as parents, give us the wisdom to make sure that the church we are attending is preaching the true biblical based gospel. In Jesus holy name, Amen

THE KING OF GLORY

The earth is the LORD's and the fullness thereof,
the world and those who dwell therein,
² for he has founded it upon the seas
and established it upon the rivers.
³ Who shall ascend the hill of the LORD?
And who shall stand in his holy place?
⁴ He who has clean hands and a pure heart,
who does not lift up his soul to what is false
and does not swear deceitfully.
⁵ He will receive blessing from the LORD
and righteousness from the God of his salvation.
⁶ Such is the generation of those who seek him,
who seek the face of the God of Jacob. *Selah*
⁷ Lift up your heads, O gates!
And be lifted up, O ancient doors,
that the King of glory may come in.
⁸ Who is this King of glory?
The LORD, strong and mighty,
the LORD, mighty in battle!
⁹ Lift up your heads, O gates!
And lift them up, O ancient doors,
that the King of glory may come in
¹⁰ Who is this King of glory?
The LORD of hosts,
he is the King of glory! *Selah*
Psalm 24

This psalm is a mighty exclamation of praise. That praise is directed precisely at God. It is a rendition of giving worship to God as the creator, sustainer and source of all power and glory.

Psalm 24 was probably used to celebrate the entry of the Ark of the Covenant into the temple built with Solomon's directions.

In later years, Psalm 24 was used as the supporting scripture to celebrate Ascension Day. The day commemorating Jesus's leaving his earthly ministry to reside at the right hand of God the Father. (Perhaps it might be used at the second resurrection.)

Whatever the reason, the use of the Psalm fits our personal role on earth to celebrate our forward-looking faith toward our eternal home.

We are all so proud of our achievements in that some of us are even planning trips into space. Our technology as inhabitants of the earth has ranged from speech, handwriting, to being able to connect even remote areas of this planet by cell phone. We deal in various forms of exchange: barter, to euro, to dollar to bitcoin.

Yet the psalmist asks us who shall ascend up to the hill of the Lord? The answer is he that has clean hands and a pure heart. Those whose sins have been erased and paid for by the death of Jesus on the cross. May all of Christ's followers see those mighty Gates of Heaven be lifted up for their final entry?

Prayer:

Father, thank you for giving King David the inspired words of Psalm 24. We lift our hands in prayer, praise and awe as we anticipate our triumphal entry into our eternal reward.

In the holy name of Jesus Christ, our Lord. Amen

THOSE YOU HAVE GIVEN TO ME

[6] "I have manifested your name to the people whom you gave me out of the world. Yours they were, and you gave them to me, and they have kept your word. [7] Now they know that everything that you have given me is from you. [8] For I have given them the words that you gave me, and they have received them and have come to know in truth that I came from you; and they have believed that you sent me. [9] I am praying for them. I am not praying for the world but for those whom you have given me, for they are yours. [10] All mine are yours, and yours are mine, and I am glorified in them.

John 17:6-10

Jesus is speaking in his final prayer while on this earth to God the Father. It is known as "The High Priestly Prayer". In this prayer, Jesus is saying goodbye to his disciples. This band of men that are closer than brothers. They have spent three years in the "Jesus Seminary". Jesus is saying that his hour has come. All throughout his three-year ministry he has often said that his hour has not yet come. Now his time on earth is drawing to a close.

Now Jesus is praying specifically for his disciples. These are the ones that the Father has given to him. These are the men who said "yes" quickly when Jesus invited them to follow him. Little did they understand that their acceptance was for the rest of their lives? A lesson for all of us is that a decision to follow Jesus is never on a trial basis or for a short time of ministry.

Jesus prays that the Father will make his disciples holy. These disciples will be made holy in a process of sanctification which is an ongoing process that ends when their mortality is ended. Just imagine that this is the blessing Jesus is asking the Father to bestow on the men that will continue the Christianity process that is still all around us to this day. Each of us should offer a prayer of thanksgiving for being able to pray and influence others to be part of the Jesus followers.

An essential part of the prayer is that the disciples will impart the truth. Our society doesn't universally endorse absolute truth. We are mandated to spread this truth that is absolute and is based upon faith.

Next on the list of Jesus' petitions is for a blessing upon those that hear the words of the disciples. Another lesson here is that the Word when shared needs always to be covered in prayer.

As you read this brief summary of certain aspects of Jesus's prayer for his disciples, he refers to them as the ones that the Father has given to him. Each one of us has a circle of friends that have been given to us. We are expected to be their spiritual leader and lift them up in prayer. Also our words and actions speak volumes for our ministry mandate. So who are the ones given to you? How about your family, friends, work contacts, golf partners, fishing friends etc. Everyone who has conversations with us has been given to us. The question remains, "how is your ministry going"?

Prayer:

Holy Father, I pray for the ones that you have given to me. My intent is to be more dedicated to their spiritual growth. I will pray for them daily and look for opportunities to minister to their spiritual and physical needs. Amen

TO LIVE IS CHRIST

²¹ For to me to live is Christ, and to die is gain. ²² If I am to live in the flesh, that means fruitful labor for me. Yet which I shall choose I cannot tell. ²³ I am hard pressed between the two. My desire is to depart and be with Christ, for that is far better. ²⁴ But to remain in the flesh is more necessary on your account.
Philippians 1:21-24

Christian heroes of the faith come to mind every time I read the texts taken from Paul's letter to the Philippians. Modern day heroes are Mother Theresa, Martin Luther King and the Billy Graham family just to name a few.

What is unique about the letter to the Philippians is that the Apostle Paul writes from a Roman prison. There is adequate proof that Paul is aware that in the next few years his life will be extinguished by the Roman government. With knowledge of his approaching role as a martyr, he still remains active and writes from his cell. He is given a gift from the Philippian church and Paul authors a letter of encouragement to the church members.

This is basically a letter of love. With his looming death ahead, Paul writes "to live is Christ and to die is gain". Paul further states that if necessary, he will continue in ministry but if given a choice he would rather go to be with the Lord.

Reading the letter to the Philippians makes me very humble when I analyze my feeble attempts at ministry. Every breath we take is a gift from God. None of us knows how long we will have the time, finances, and physical ability to be involved in living for Christ.

The times that we are living in are experiencing moral decay. We need to be very astute in how we spend our finances and energies in our opportunities to support the kingdom of Christ. Now more than ever, we need to evaluate what we are supporting. Some good questions to ask before you spend support monies are what percentage of your dollar is being spent on the cause being advertised? Is the educational institution graduating young people who believe in the United States as being a desirable place to live and raise a family? Does the Christian college hold to the Bible? You get the idea, be cautious in how you live for Christ.

Prayer:
Father God, give me a questioning mind to do my best to support your kingdom causes with my time and finances. Once I have decided to give, give me a generous heart that keeps giving of what you have given me back to your kingdom. In Jesus name, Amen

UNDER CONSTRUCTION

*[10] According to the grace of God given to me, like a
skilled[a] master builder I laid a foundation,
and someone else is building upon it. Let each one take
care how he builds upon it. [11] For no one can lay
a foundation other than that which is laid, which is
Jesus Christ. [12] Now if anyone builds on the foundation
with gold, silver, precious stones, wood, hay,
straw— [13] each one's work will become manifest, for the
Day will disclose it, because it will be revealed by fire,
and the fire will test what sort of work each one has
done. [14] If the work that anyone has built on the
foundation survives, he will receive a reward. [15] If
anyone's work is burned up, he will suffer loss, though
he himself will be saved, but only as through fire.
[16] Do you not know that you[b] are God's temple and that
God's Spirit dwells in you? [17] If anyone destroys God's
temple, God will destroy him. For God's temple is holy,
and you are that temple.
1 Corinthians 3:10-17*

Being a bachelor at age 74 was a unique
experience for me. My wife of 54 blessed years went on
to her eternal home in glory. After three months of
keeping myself busy with interior painting of my home,
my daughter gave me some sage advice: "Dad, why don't
you do some woodworking? When my boys were
younger, they spent hours on the rocking horse that you
built?" So I proceeded to outfit a workshop in my
unfinished basement.

A good friend of mine who had many years of woodworking experience offered to become my mentor. That relationship developed into a close friendship and in many ways a soul mate. My daughter in law asked me to build a dining room table. It took us a few years, marked by laughter, marginal comments and finally a very presentable table. The table was made of red oak and measured 3" x 8'. My son and his sons moved it out of the basement to their home in Kalamazoo. Now we're into toy boxes made out of cherry wood.

So much for wood. On a spiritual level, we are all projects under construction. We can gain deeper insights when we can open our hearts to a soul mate that will listen and nudge us in a correct direction when we have doubts and questions in our personal lives. A soul mate can make sure we are measured, planed and sanded in our spiritual lives.

The table is now completed, but the temple is still under construction. Does your temple need some constructive changes? You are a holy creation and God lives within you. Your family and peers are observing your life and some are following your example. You just might be the construction foreman.

Prayer:
Father today I'm evaluating my temple. It's not perfect. In fact it has some hidden flaws. Mold me and make me after your will. I'm yours, totally and completely. In Jesus name, Amen

WHAT FLOATS YOUR BOAT?

[20] For when you were slaves of sin, you were free in regard to righteousness. [21] But what fruit were you getting at that time from the things of which you are now ashamed? For the end of those things is death. [22] But now that you have been set free from sin and have become slaves of God, the fruit you get leads to sanctification and its end, eternal life. [23] For the wages of sin is death, but the free gift of God is eternal life in Christ Jesus our Lord.
Romans 6:20-23

Recently, one of the world's largest container ships got stuck crosswise in the Suez Canal. Apparently, high desert winds had turned the 1,300 ft. vessel and it became stuck and because of its huge size blocked the canal to all large ships. Many ships were rerouted around South Africa because they couldn't wait to be unloaded.

Crews were removing millions of feet of sand from under the massive ship named Ever Given. Twice the pulling cables snapped under the extreme stress of the tugging effort. A Dutch team by the name of Smit was brought in and their solution was to offload the massive cargo of some 18,000 containers. This idea was deemed impractical. The most powerful tugboat available with the pulling power of about 285 metric tons was engaged and together with the lifting effect of a Supermoon tide which raised water levels by 19 inches finally freed the huge vessel.

Supermoon tides occur when the full moon coincides when it is closest to the earth during its elliptical orbit. So without the forces created by our God the boat would have stayed stuck for a much longer period of time.

How does the story of a stuck container ship fit into a book of meditations? Yes, the author is fascinated with boats. The real reason is that we often get into situations where we are stuck in our lives and there seems to be no solution available. Only God can free you from the difficulties in life that are keeping you stuck. Jesus died on the cross and paid for all your past, present and future sins that are keeping you immobile and mentally at your wit's end.

You don't have to wait for an extreme event to free you from the difficulties of your present life. Just ask Jesus into your heart and life, confess your past sins and pledge to live a life devoted to Jesus and his service for the future.

Begin your personal prayer here if you feel the nudge to do so. Blessings on your relationship with your heavenly Father

WHAT IS IT GOING TO TAKE?

*Now the whole earth had one language and the same
words. [2] And as people migrated from the east, they
found a plain in the land of Shinar and settled there. [3]
And they said to one another, "Come, let us make
bricks, and burn them thoroughly." And they had brick
for stone, and bitumen for mortar[4] then they said
"Come let us build a city and a tower with its top in the
heavens, and let us make a name for ourselves lest we
be dispersed over the face of the whole earth." [5] And
the Lord came down to see the city and tower, which the
children of man had built. [6] And the Lord said, "Behold
they are one people, and they have one language, and
this is only the beginning of what they will do. And
nothing that they propose to do will be impossible for
them.[7] Come let us go down and confuse their language,
so that they may not understand one another's speech."
[8] So the Lord dispersed them from there over the face of
the earth, and they left off building the city. [9] Therefore
its name was Babel, because there the Lord confused
the language of all the earth. And from there the Lord
dispersed them over the face of all the earth.*
Genesis 11:1-9

In the beginning of the earth some principles had
to be established so that man could understand that God
was supreme, and that man was in a unique position of
service to God.

Genesis clearly states that there is only one God.
Creation came into being by the voice commands of God.

Man needed to understand that God would not tolerate sin and the flood was the result.

Later, the tower of Babel showed man that even though he had devised an excellent building method composed of sun-dried bricks and straw, bricks held in position with bitumen, there needed to be a dispersion of all of mankind. So, God established many diverse languages and dialects which stopped easy communication and consequently the building project came to an abrupt halt.

At the early establishment of life on earth, God used some very basic incidents to depict that God was supreme and that man was totally dependent upon God.

The events at the beginning of time were the creation, the Garden of Eden, the fall of man, the flood and the tower of Babel. The unspoken question but clearly defined question posed by all of these events is that God was asking man, "What is it going to take?" What will it take for you to understand that I am God and that you are man and we are a family in a divine sense?

God is still asking the same question, "What is it going to take?" The events in our lives are being allowed by God to get our attention to the events in our lives that make us stop and realize that we are not the captains of our own souls in entirety. We are faced with peaks and valleys in our finances, our health and our relationships.

Perhaps it's time in our prayers to realize that they are not solely our petitions but are in a deeper sense a time of communication. We need to divest ourselves of the baggage that clouds our prayers and realize that in all of life there is an ongoing question which can be postponed but never avoided. God is asking "What will it take for you to come to me completely?"

Prayer:

Father, forgive our sins of thinking that we are in total charge of our lives. We give you adoration in that we know that nothing happens in our lives without your awareness. So give us the patience to slow down and have a "heart to heart" conversation with you regarding the towers that we think we are building but realize that you are in total charge of things and we bow down in worship. Amen

TAMING THE TONGUE

Not many of you should become teachers, my brothers, for you know that we who teach will be judged with greater strictness. ² For we all stumble in many ways. And if anyone does not stumble in what he says, he is a perfect man, able also to bridle his whole body. ³ If we put bits into the mouths of horses so that they obey us, we guide their whole bodies as well. ⁴ Look at the ships also: though they are so large and are driven by strong winds, they are guided by a very small rudder wherever the will of the pilot directs. ⁵ So also the tongue is a small member, yet it boasts of great things.

How great a forest is set ablaze by such a small fire! ⁶ And the tongue is a fire, a world of unrighteousness. The tongue is set among our members, staining the whole body, setting on fire the entire course of life, and set on fire by hell ⁷ For every kind of beast and bird, of reptile and sea creature, can be tamed and has been tamed by mankind, ⁸ but no human being can tame the tongue. It is a restless evil, full of deadly poison. ⁹ With it we bless our Lord and Father, and with it we curse people who are made in the likeness of God. ¹⁰ From the same mouth come blessing and cursing. My brothers these things ought not to be so. ¹¹ Does a spring pour forth from the same opening both fresh and salt water? ¹² Can a fig tree, my brothers, bear olives, or a grapevine produce figs? Neither can a salt pond yield fresh water.
James 3: 1-12

In today's society it is quite often that various friends gather to enjoy a "coffee break". It is at these gatherings that opinions and various historical facts get rehashed, somewhat embellished and brought to light for all to hear. Sadly however, many of the discussions have a tendency to place emphasis on the negative facts concerning a person or family who has experienced problems in finances, marital strife or family discord.

Seldom does one hear the positive aspects of one's life such as their donations of time and or money. We seldom hear about their visits to the lonely or to the ill.

I'm wondering if there were coffee or wine breaks during biblical times. How do you suppose they would remember King David? Would they recall his affair with Bathsheba and the murder of her husband? Possibly even the death of the son resulting from the affair. Would the Apostle Paul be remembered for his part in the stoning of Stephen? How about Paul arranging for the torture of new Christians?

You get the idea. How about remembering the positive aspects in lieu of negative facts. I love conversations about how someone has conquered their addictions. How a family is back on the road to healing in their finances would be good to hear. How about relating a story of your latest interaction with someone you are trying to lead to the gospel? Such conversations just might be "In the Net" experiences.

Prayer:
Father, forgive our times of delight in engaging in gossip. Instead, move our conversations to relate our love for others. In Jesus name, Amen.

TRUTH

17 Sanctify them in the truth; your word is truth. 18 As you sent me into the world, so I have sent them into the world. 19 And for their sake I consecrate myself,[b] that they also may be sanctified[c] in truth.
20 "I do not ask for these only, but also for those who will believe in me through their word, 21 that they may all be one, just as you, Father, are in me, and I in you, that they also may be in us, so that the world may believe that you have sent me.
John 17: 17-21

At a small Christian college, my initial course in philosophy posed the question, "what is absolute truth?" The premise of the question was to get us underclassmen to think through the questions of life.

The questioning of authority has become commonplace since the Vietnamese War. Patriotism was openly questioned for the first time in the public square.

However, the question of what constitutes truth was questioned by Pontius Pilate at the hearing concerning Jesus' teaching when Pilate questioned Jesus by asking "What is Truth"?

In the movie, "A Few Good Men," Jack Nicholson snarls at Tom Cruise stating, "You can't handle the truth".

Jesus in his "High Priestly Prayer" asked the Father to sanctify his disciples in the truth. Jesus further stated that your word is truth. The fact is that the word of

God does not conform to an external standard of truth because it is the absolute standard of truth in and of itself. So everything else in life needs to be held up to the ultimate standard of truth, God's word.

Our society has reduced the absolutes of the truth to questioning and/or at best given them a status of "maybe".

Back to Jack Nicholson, "can we handle the truth?" It is our spiritual calling to handle the absolute truth and thereby assist others in their personal process of sanctification.

Prayer:
Father, I need your direction in letting others know that your word is the absolute truth. May my demeanor be loving and caring and so let others know that you and your word are absolutely true. Amen

Suggestion: read the entire High Priestly Prayer which Jesus prayed to God the Father and is found in John 17.

ASSURANCE

¹ Now faith is the assurance of things hoped for, the conviction of things not seen. ² For by it the people of old received their commendation. ³ By faith we understand that the universe was created by the word of God, so that what is seen was not made out of things that are visible.

Hebrews 11: 1-3

Assurance is not a vague hope but a full confidence that something in the future, not seen, but which has been promised by God, will come to pass. This confidence is based upon the biblical promise that if we place our faith in God who fully backs his promises because he is forever trustworthy. God has promised that he will never forsake his own.

A "soul mate" friend of mine posed the question as to "what is the origin of faith"? He thinks deeply and is very much "into the Word". The question cannot and should not be flippantly answered. I left the conversation without a definitive answer and it has been ruminating about in my mind for a rather long period of time.

Soon there will be another lunch with my very dear friend, and I have a more precise answer for him. My response will be something like the following brief explanation drawn from my own personal life's journey.

The story begins with a new location because of a career change. We were living in Traverse City and things were going nicely. We were in a friendly neighborhood and our church home was warm and biblically rock solid. (Our pastor was the late Warren Burgess) who was an absolute saint and just what we needed at this mid-point in our lives. Then everything changed.

Our family experienced six deaths over a two-year period. The last death was that of our oldest son, Mike. He never made it home from work one summer evening in August. A head – on traffic accident being the cause. Many years later the memories surrounding this point in our lives causes my very heart to clinch and for a tear to moisten my script.

So, faith for me has been and is best described as being on a continuum with hope at the left side and rock-solid assurance (faith) at the right. In between, there have been fluctuations based upon life's experiences and my perceptions of them.

Simply stated, faith in God ranges from wishy washy hope mixed with doubts to a rock-solid assurance of true faith in our creator, redeemer and source of our faith which rises and falls with the experiences of our lives.

What has worked in my life when I am overcome with doubts is that my prayers take on a greater depth. I also find solace especially in the Psalms. Psalm 30:5C states that: "weeping may tarry for the night, but joy comes with the morning."

So, at my next lunch with my friend, I'll give him a summation of this writing. Without a doubt, the topic will be discussed in detail and probably cause me to make minor corrections to my writing. However, the writing of Hebrews will be the source of our discussion.

The question on the table at the close of this writing is where are you regarding your assurance? Is it a weak hope or is it a solid faith? One thing is for sure, that God has allowed you to experience many peaks and valleys upon your journey toward eternity. It is my desire that you are solid in your assurance of faith.

Prayer: *Father, listen to your children praying at this moment. Move us toward the words of the hymn:*

Blessed Assurance

Blessed assurance, Jesus is mine!

Oh, what a foretaste of glory divine!

Heir of salvation, purchase of God,

Born of his Spirit, washed in his blood

Refrain

This is my story, this is my song,

Praising my Savior all the day long.

This is my story, this is my song,

Praising my Savior all the day long.

Amen

BLESSING

[24] The LORD bless you and keep you;
[25] the LORD make his face to shine upon you and be
gracious to you;
[26] the LORD lift up his countenance upon you and give
you peace.
Numbers 6: 24-26

This blessing which God gave to Moses who directed Aaron to bless the Israelites has been sung by choirs as a doxology. It is a beautiful piece of music and speaks to one's soul.

In some circles it is known as Aaron's Blessing or the Priestly Blessing. God blessed the Israelites by a successful exodus from Egypt to the promised land. In addition, they were blessed with good harvests, many offspring, peace and above all the presence of God. This presence was symbolized in the Ark of the Covenant, in the leading to the promised land by fire at night and a cloud by daylight.

Jesus spent the core of his Sermon on the Mount with emphasis on blessing as listed in the Beatitudes:

[3] "Blessed are the poor in spirit, for theirs is the
kingdom of heaven.
[4] "Blessed are those who mourn, for they shall be
comforted.
[5] "Blessed are the meek, for they shall inherit the earth.
[6] "Blessed are those who hunger and thirst for
righteousness, for they shall be satisfied.

[7] "Blessed are the merciful, for they shall receive mercy.
[8] "Blessed are the pure in heart, for they shall see God.
[9] "Blessed are the peacemakers, for they shall be
called sons of God.
[10] "Blessed are those who are persecuted for
righteousness' sake, for theirs is the kingdom of heaven.
[11] "Blessed are you when others revile you and
persecute you and utter all kinds of evil against you
falsely on my account. [12] Rejoice and be glad, for your
reward is great in heaven, for so they persecuted the
prophets who were before you.
Matthew 5: 3-12

The word blessing is used in modern day circles quite freely and often flippantly. However, the use of a blessing is often overlooked in everyday life. Why not let others know that they have been a blessing in your life? Also, when we approve of a new relationship, let the persons involved know that they have your blessing. Perhaps a bit old fashioned but often overlooked in today's society.

Let your spouse know that she is a blessing in your marriage. Her loving ways are often taken for granted. Your children need to hear that they are blessed. This will bring light and joy to those upon whom you render a blessing. What a way to let others know that we are Jesus' ambassadors.

Prayer: Father you have blessed us and perhaps we have taken your favor of blessing for granted. Now we just want to extend your blessing to others that need to hear from you. May it be done through us. Amen

Business Plan

¹³ Come now, you who say, "Today or tomorrow we will go into such and such a town and spend a year there and trade and make a profit"— ¹⁴ yet you do not know what tomorrow will bring. What is your life? For you are a mist that appears for a little time and then vanishes. ¹⁵ Instead you ought to say, "If the Lord wills, we will live and do this or that." ¹⁶ As it is, you boast in your arrogance. All such boasting is evil. ¹⁷ So whoever knows the right thing to do and fails to do it, for him it is sin.

James 4:13-17

What is your business plan is the key question asked by bankers and venture capitalists when an individual asks for a loan or for a line of credit?

However, no one knows for sure what the future will bring. We can't know for sure about our future because God has not revealed to us what the future will bring. Each person is one heartbeat away from eternity. So, is it wrong to plan for our futures? Or should we just live our lives without any sort of plan for the future?

Each one of us has cognitive skills that give us the ability to predict the future to the best of our mortal ability. Of course, we should then plan for the future to the best of our abilities. We will then submit our business plan after carefully looking at all the pros and cons that we can realistically predict what our future might hold.

However, the future is always the unforeseen such as a pandemic, recession, marriage failure, or accident that can drastically alter your plans.

Conversely, what are your plans for your immortal existence after you die? Each one of us will surely leave this life. Have you submitted your plan for life after death? You really can't put it off. None of us knows when we will cease to exist here on earth. We don't know what God has planned for us. Therefore, it is absolutely necessary for us to plan our immortal "business plan". Many of you have maybe planned for your last days in the form or a will and/or trust. Some have perhaps planned their funerals, and some have even prepaid for them. Others even have a burial plot reserved complete with a headstone. At death, your soul will leave your body and will reside in a destination of your selection. Have you made that eternal "business plan?"

Prayer: Father, I've always wanted to go to heaven when I die. I have not made the arrangements. Please forgive my sinful past and accept me into your present and eternal kingdom. Amen

CHARIOTS

*⁹ When they had crossed, Elijah said to Elisha, "Ask
what I shall do for you, before I am taken from you."
And Elisha said, "Please let there be a double portion
of your spirit on me." ¹⁰ And he said, "You have asked a
hard thing; yet, if you see me as I am being taken from
you, it shall be so for you, but if you do not see me, it
shall not be so." ¹¹ And as they still went on and talked,
behold, chariots of fire and horses of fire separated the
two of them. And Elijah went up by a whirlwind into
heaven. ¹² And Elisha saw it and he cried, "My father,
my father! The chariots of Israel and its horsemen!"
And he saw him no more.
II Kings 2: 9-12a*

Chariots have always held a special place in my spiritual
thinking. My cousin, Larry first made me aware of the
significance of what he called the "great chariot ride"
when he was referring to and anticipating his eternal
reward. I've always imagined that his chariot was a
special one because of the many souls he had introduced
to the kingdom of heaven.

It all started out when Elijah was mentoring Elisha at the
end of Elijah's life here on earth. At the end of their
parting conversation, chariots of fire and horses of fire
appeared, and Elijah was transported in a whirlwind
directly into heaven. What a symbol of God's power and
immediate blessing! Elisha is so overcome that he cries

out, "My father, my father! The chariots of Israel and its horsemen!" Elisha has Elijah's cloak (mantel) which was a symbol of Elijah's power being transferred to Elisha. Elisha casts that same cloak upon the Jordan River and immediately the waters backed up and Elisha walked across the Jordan on a dry riverbed.

Someday each one of us will take a "great chariot ride." That ride will take place the moment of your last breath. Are you assured where your chariot is headed? In Philippians 1:22-24 it is clearly stated that a follower of Jesus will go directly to be with Jesus.

Prayer:

Swing Low Sweet Chariot

Comin for to carry me home.

I'm sometimes up and sometimes down

Comin for to carry me home

But I know my soul is heaven bound

Comin for to carry me home.

Amen

CHILD DISCIPLINE

Whoever spares the rod hates his son,
but he who loves him is diligent to discipline him.

Proverbs 13:24

Child rearing today for the most part is far more physically gentle than in prior generations. Today spanking is most unusual and is viewed by many as child abuse. Instead, a "time out" is quite often the punishment for a youngster whose behavior needs adjustment.

In the Bible, the rod was often used as a means of discipline. The rod was a slim stick quite similar to a paint stirring stick of modern day.

Catholic schools quite often used a ruler to strike a student's hands when his behavior needed to be adjusted.

My generation (senior citizen) can remember that spanking was often used. A friend of mine had a leather strop used for honing straight edge razors upon which he had printed "I need thee every hour". The results of spanking were usually immediate in the form of tears and changed behavior.

Personally, when I was about seven years old, I announced to my mother that I was moving to my buddy Paul's house because their atmosphere was more to my liking. She even helped me pack by putting necessary items into a large red handkerchief which I knotted and inserted a sturdy stick, put it over my shoulder and proceeded to march to Paul's house. I had traveled for about 15 minutes when my older sister pulled alongside me on her bike. Her words turned me around immediately because when she said that mom was frying chicken for supper and that was my favorite meal. I was greeted by my mom who had the green shoots from a fig tree stump in her hand. These were applied to my backside with her muttering words sounding like "never again". The welts subsided; the words remained permanently etched in my little boy's heart. After that session, Paul's house is by special invitation and approved by both moms.

My senior citizen ideas of child rearing are not to attempt to tell others on how to raise their children. Every home has their own methods. My singular input is to not overdo a particular method. If you occasionally spank, do so out of love and not your own personal anger. Non conditional love needs to be the theme of child rearing. Our heavenly father has so loved us without condition and purely out of grace.

Prayer: Father give me a cool head as I discipline my children. May my behavior reflect how you have and are loving me with pure grace. Amen

CONTENTMENT

He who loves money will not be satisfied with money,
nor he who loves wealth with his income.
Ecclesiastes 5:10
No one can serve two masters, for either he will hate the
one and love the other, or he will be devoted to the one
and despise the other. You cannot serve God and money.
Matthew 6:24
But those who desire to be rich fall into temptation, into
a snare, into many senseless and harmful desires that
plunge people into ruin and destruction.10 For the love
of money is the root of all kinds of evils. It is through
this craving that some have wandered away from the
faith and pierced themselves with many pangs.
I Timothy 6:9-10
Keep your life free from the love of money, and be
content with what you have, for he has said, "I will
never leave you nor forsake you."
Hebrews 13:5

Money has been a key factor in the futuristic thinking efforts in the city in which I live. Philanthropy by wealthy individuals has developed medicine, the arts and general business climate to a point of enviable excellence.

For contentment to exist, the love of money cannot be present. So what is the difference between the love of money and contentment? There is no magical formula or equation that can answer the question "how much is enough?"

Those with great wealth that are actively blessing civic endeavors, Christian causes, and funding efforts to be obedient to the Great Commission are examples of money stewardship and will be able to "go through the eye of a needle" into their eternal reward. Money has not been their love. The kingdom of God has been their passion and consequently their one source of contentment.

To those who seriously question what constitutes the love of money should analyze their level of giving to causes of God's kingdom by setting up a simple balance sheet with two columns.

Net Worth   Kingdom Donations

The result of your analysis will probably be like our response when we are asked similar questions at the great judgment.

Parting light thought; it is not a sin to have adequate resources to fund possible assisted living and/or nursing home care. However, it's not necessary to set aside enough assets to buy the institution.

Go with God and do not let greed shadow your contentment.

Prayer: Father you are my "All in All". Give me contentment with your assets that you have given to me temporarily to increase your kingdom. Amen

CUP

⁵ The LORD is my chosen portion and my cup;
you hold my lot.
⁶ The lines have fallen for me in pleasant places;
indeed, I have a beautiful inheritance.
Psalm 16: 5-6

When one refers to their cup it can literally mean their portion. The psalmist, David spoke to his personal satisfaction with God's portion or cup that he had been given in life. In today's society it is quite unusual for people to express their comfort in God's providential care. Instead, we are surrounded by a general clamor of individuals that want more and more. We seldom hear expressions of thankful people who are living a life of gratitude.

Going on, each one of us has been given a cup. That is, we are at a place in our lives that we have many available options as to what to do with the cup of blessing given to us by God. Simple acts such as showing love to a child as stated in Matthew 23:25,26. Yes just a cup of cold water is an act of love.

- *Woe to you, scribes and Pharisees, hypocrites! For you clean the outside of the cup and the plate, but inside they are full of greed and self-indulgence.*
- *You blind Pharisee! First clean the inside of the cup and the plate, that the outside may also be clean.*

In Matthew 23 Jesus takes the scribes and Pharisees to task in that he exposes the phony religious acts as shallow and specifically designed to gain the applause of others. Again, the subject of a cup comes up but in a totally different manner. When David was grateful for his cup or portion it was a symbol of God's blessing upon his life. By contrast, when Jesus spoke of a cup in relation to the scribes and Pharisees, the cup was pointed out as a symbol of hypocrisy. Jesus said that you clean the outside of the cup until it gleams. Others by observation will only see the outside of the beautiful cup but inside it is full of greed and self-indulgence.

You and I have been given a portion of blessings which is symbolized as our "cup". Are you thanking God for your portion as David? Or are you just showing a shiny exterior? Take just a moment of silence and look inward. How is your cup?

Prayer: Father, thank you for my cup of blessing. Today I will look more carefully at the inside of my cup and take an effort to clean up my cup so that all can see you through me. Amen

CURTAIN

^{51} And behold, the curtain of the temple was torn in two, from top to bottom. And the earth shook, and the rocks were split. ^{52} The tombs also were opened. And many bodies of the saints who had fallen asleep were raised, ^{53} and coming out of the tombs after his resurrection they went into the holy city and appeared to many. ^{54} When the centurion and those who were with him, keeping watch over Jesus, saw the earthquake and what took place, they were filled with awe and said, "Truly this was the Son of God!"

Matthew 27: 51-54

Curtains in our lives are decorative and are meant to be pleasing and complimentary additions to the décor of the room. By contrast, the Temple of Herod, which was in existence during the time of Jesus, featured a massive curtain which separated the Holy Place from the Most Holy Place. This curtain was 62 feet high and 30 feet wide. It was elaborately woven of 72 plaits which consisted of twisted 24 threads each. The high priest could only enter the Most Holy Place once per year to sprinkle incense and blood to atone for the sins of the people.

This curtain was torn in two during Jesus' crucifixion. Its significance symbolized the separation between God and his people was now nonexistent. The power of the crucifixion was further symbolized by splitting rocks and saints rising from their graves. Regular earthquakes do not split rocks, open graves, resurrect deceased bodies, and split heavy intricately woven fabric. No wonder the centurion and those with him who were guarding the crucifixion were moved to exclaim. "truly this was the Son of God!"

19 Therefore, brothers, since we have confidence to enter the holy places by the blood of Jesus, 20 by the new and living way that he opened for us through the curtain, that is, through his flesh, 21 and since we have a great priest over the house of God, 22 let us draw near with a true heart in full assurance of faith, with our hearts sprinkled clean from an evil conscience and our bodies washed with pure water. 23 Let us hold fast the confession of our hope without wavering, for he who promised is faithful. 24 And let us consider how to stir up one another to love and good works, 25 not neglecting to meet together, as is the habit of some, but encouraging one another, and all the more as you see the Day drawing near.

Hebrews 10:19-25

Perhaps some of us have doubts about the crucifixion of Jesus. Some questions which might be asked are "did the crucifixion really take away my sin?" The excerpt from Hebrews answers the question about the power of the crucifixion. The temple curtain was torn in two and the symbolism of that tearing of cloth gives us confidence to enter the Most Holy Place. Yes, there are no more dividers. We have direct access to the throne of God through the power of prayer. Our sins have been accounted for on the cross of Jesus. There is nothing that stands in the way of our adoration and praise.

This is a mind-blowing part of our salvation. No more barriers. No curtain. Just you and God. Let's go to him now in prayer.

Prayer: Father, thank you for making my sins be accounted for by the power of the crucifixion. I am in awe. I worship you and want to make every day a day of thankful living. Amen

ETERNITY

Truly, truly, I say to you, whoever hears my word and believes him who sent me has eternal life. He does not come into judgement but has passed from death to life.
John 5:24

I write these things to you who believe in the name of the Son of God, that you may know that you have eternal life. I John 5:13

⁹ What gain has the worker from his toil? ¹⁰ I have seen the business that God has given to the children of man to be busy with. ¹¹ He has made everything beautiful in its time. Also, he has put eternity into man's heart, yet so that he cannot find out what God has done from the beginning to the end. ¹² I perceived that there is nothing better for them than to be joyful and to do good as long as they live; ¹³ also that everyone should eat and drink and take pleasure in all his toil—this is God's gift to man.
Ecclesiastes 3:9-13

Eternity is a topic that man can't begin to describe because as man understands the concept of time there is a beginning and an end. However, eternity as depicted in the Bible is without beginning or end. Consequently, we are now involved in eternity. The eternity of one who hears the gospel and believes is presently in process!

The second scripture found in I John goes a step further. It plainly says that you who believe in the name of the Son of God will know that you now have eternal life. Yes, now here on earth, you are experiencing the beginning of eternal life. At death, our souls will join others who have gone on before us to the glorious extension of our eternity. When one goes back to examine the original Greek language the word eternal not only indicates length to life but also quality. Right now, as a believer you are experiencing the initial quality of eternity that will be in glory beyond description and will have no end!

One of the more vibrant churches that I'm somewhat familiar with recently went through an in-depth analysis of their ministry. The evaluator looked at all the facets of ministry including preaching, education, parking, security, attendance gains and losses etc. were just some of the points covered in the evaluation. A particular issue raised by the analysis pointed out that the church as a whole is convinced that eternal life in heaven was where they were heading at death. However, they did not appear to be living a joyful life here on earth.

The writer of Ecclesiastes (probably Solomon) said virtually the same thing as the church evaluator pointed out. The scripture says that you live in a beautiful creation and God has put eternity within your hearts. Therefore, enjoy the part of eternity that you are now experiencing and celebrate. Enjoy this day! It is the day the Lord has made. Let us rejoice and be glad in it. Psalm 118:24

Prayer: Father, we have failed to celebrate the beginning of our eternity in our present time on earth. May we take special efforts to live a joyful life that others may see you living within us. Amen

HEART CHECK

[10] And he called the people to him and said to them, "Hear and understand: [11] it is not what goes into the mouth that defiles a person, but what comes out of the mouth; this defiles a person." [12] Then the disciples came and said to him, "Do you know that the Pharisees were offended when they heard this saying?" [13] He answered, "Every plant that my heavenly Father has not planted will be rooted up. [14] Let them alone; they are blind guides.[a] And if the blind lead the blind, both will fall into a pit." [15] But Peter said to him, "Explain the parable to us." [16] And he said, "Are you also still without understanding? [17] Do you not see that whatever goes into the mouth passes into the stomach and is expelled?[b] [18] But what comes out of the mouth proceeds from the heart, and this defiles a person. [19] For out of the heart come evil thoughts, murder, adultery, sexual immorality, theft, false witness, slander. [20] These are what defile a person. But to eat with unwashed hands does not defile anyone."

Matthew 15: 10-20

Today, heart disease is one of the leading causes of death in the USA. We are a nation that is basically number one globally in our standard of living. We can eat almost anything because we can afford it. Eating an unhealthy amount and type of food and lack of exercise appear to be the main contributing factors to heart disease.

What about our spiritual hearts? What defiles a person's heart? Our scripture of today explains very completely that it is out of our hearts that come all of our words and actions. Our thoughts lead us to action and speaking. So where is your heart? If you have impure thoughts, what have you done about it? Have you acted out those thoughts and asked for forgiveness or are you living a life that is motivated by impure thoughts and you have concluded that you might as well go on living without moral restrictions because you just can't be forgiven?

Jesus has the answer for you. He and he alone can forgive all your impure thoughts and actions. Just ask him to take over your heart and he will forgive all of your sins of the past, present and future. Once you give yourself over to Jesus, all of your past is over. No more regrets and feelings of guilt. Jesus died on the cross and arose from the dead to conquer sin for everyone who gives their heart over to him. So friend, where are you at? Where's your heart? Jesus is knocking at the door of your life. Do you hear him?

Prayer: Jesus, you paid the price for all of the sins in the world. Please accept my plea for your mercy and forgiveness. I want to serve you from now on. Amen

HOPE

18 For I consider that the sufferings of this present time are not worth comparing with the glory that is to be revealed to us. 19 For the creation waits with eager longing for the revealing of the sons of God. 20 For the creation was subjected to futility, not willingly, but because of him who subjected it, in hope 21 that the creation itself will be set free from its bondage to corruption and obtain the freedom of the glory of the children of God. 22 For we know that the whole creation has been groaning together in the pains of childbirth until now. 23 And not only the creation, but we ourselves, who have the first fruits of the Spirit, groan inwardly as we wait eagerly for adoption as sons, the redemption of our bodies. 24 For in this hope we were saved. Now hope that is seen is not hope. For who hopes for what he sees? 25 But if we hope for what we do not see, we wait for it with patience.
Romans 8:18-25

Wherever you are at right now, do you have hope? More clearly, are you waiting for a time when your situation will be improved?

Many of us hope for a variety of things and/or situations. Some are waiting to get married or to have our situation change so that marriage is more predictable. Others are waiting for family dynamics to change so that relationships can improve. Others are hoping for a job or for a better job. We need more money, and our working conditions are very unenjoyable to say the least.

Most of our hoping is for positive results that we can already predict and visualize. So our hope is possibly coveting what is sinful and unattainable. This level of hoping is more like wishful thinking in that we hope for goals that are beyond our physical realm because we are limited by money concerns or we are hoping for something sinful.

The hope referred to in today's scripture is on a totally different level. We can't see or imagine the hope that is being sought after. It is our ultimate hope of what will be our role in the second resurrection. Christ will physically return; bodies will come out of their graves. These bodies will be restored in a glorified form. This is our ultimate hope. This hope can't be described because if we knew exactly the details of the second resurrection it wouldn't truly be hope in its purest form.

Where are you at? Do you hope for Jesus to return or does that thought cause you great fear? Are your fears based upon doubts that you don't know for sure where your eternal home will be? You can be sure if you give over your life to Jesus as you savior. You can pray right now for Jesus to forgive all your past and present sins. When you have made that request, then promise to turn your life around and serve Jesus in your thoughts, actions and words. In so doing you now have more than just hope. You have assurance. You have faith. Welcome home! Amen

I CAN'T HEAR YOU

[14] Indeed, in their case the prophecy of Isaiah is fulfilled
that says:
""""You will indeed hear but never understand,
and you will indeed see but never perceive."
[15] For this people's heart has grown dull,
and with their ears they can barely hear,
and their eyes they have closed,
lest they should see with their eyes
and hear with their ears
and understand with their heart
and turn, and I would heal them.'
[16] But blessed are your eyes, for they see, and your ears,
for they hear.
Matthew 13:14-16

We hear God through reading his word. In addition, we hear God through bible-based preaching. Sometimes, we hear God through the words and/or actions of others.

Within each of us is an inner voice that speaks to our inner self (our soul). This is a vital aspect to hearing. We can hear but not really internalize what is being said. Another way of hearing is to really pay attention and then to respond positively in words or actions to the spiritual advice or information.

Many of us hear but we don't obey. Instead, we go our own way and pretend that what we are doing is okay, but we really know better. An illustration that follows came from a conversation I recently had with a friend.

121

This friend was wading in the lake in front of his summer home and noticed his two-year-old grandson, Christopher, walking on the neighbor's dock and not wearing the required life jacket which was in direct violation of grandpa and grandma's rule that youngsters up to a certain age must wear life jackets when walking on the docks. Grandpa immediately called "Christopher you need to put on a life jacket". Christopher didn't even look toward his grandpa but kept on walking. Grandpa again called out "Christopher" in an outdoor voice. (retired educators do not lose volume with age). Christopher continued his own way and grandpa yelled "Christopher stop and get on a life jacket!" Christopher never looked at grandpa but responded with great clarity" grandpa, I can't hear you!"

Today, as you walk along on the dock of the journey of your life, do you have on your life jacket? Simply stated, do you know for sure that heaven is your destination? If you have any doubt, Jesus will welcome you with open arms regardless of your past non hearing behavior. It's time to listen, to hear and to ask Jesus into your life.

Prayer: Father some of us are going through the motions but we need assurance. Give us that faith as we come to your invitation with hearing ears and loving hearts. Amen

LISTEN, OBEY AND TEACH

[9] "Only take care, and keep your soul diligently, lest you forget the things that your eyes have seen, and lest they depart from your heart all the days of your life. Make them known to your children and your children's children— [10] how on the day that you stood before the LORD your God at Horeb, the LORD said to me, 'Gather the people to me, that I may let them hear my words, so that they may learn to fear me all the days that they live on the earth, and that they may teach their children so.' [11] And you came near and stood at the foot of the mountain, while the mountain burned with fire to the heart of heaven, wrapped in darkness, cloud, and gloom. [12] Then the LORD spoke to you out of the midst of the fire. You heard the sound of words, but saw no form; there was only a voice. [13] And he declared to you his covenant, which he commanded you to perform, that is, the Ten Commandments,[a] and he wrote them on two tablets of stone. [14] And the LORD commanded me at that time to teach you statutes and rules, that you might do them in the land that you are going over to possess.
Deuteronomy 4: 9-14

Moses is giving a speech of exhortation to Israel. In doing so, he wants them to take heed and obey. Moses wants the Israelites to remember how that their God has cared for them through the release from the cruel Pharaoh, crossing the Red Sea and all the other great stories of the Exodus.

Even though God has denied Moses entry into the promised land, Moses remains positive in his attitude. A lesson in attitude for us can be learned from Moses in that he does not show any negative behavior in being denied entry into the promised land. He seems content that he can visually see into the promised land, from the top of Mt. Nebo. It would have been expected that Moses would have pleaded with God to allow him entry after all he went through in leading the very negative people on the Exodus.

Some questions come to mind. Do your children know the spiritual impact that you experienced when you went through some of life's severe trials? Of special interest are the spiritual issues that our country is experiencing. There is a definite culture shift taking place.

Where are you in the spiritual leadership of your children? We can't afford to put off the conversations of how we as Christians view our changing culture. God instructed Moses to make sure that the Israelites would never forget their heritage of the Exodus and all the situations associated with the long trek.

The passing on of our roots and the trials of our lives need to be passed on to the next generation. We cannot leave this culture to change without our Christian influence upon our families.

Prayer:

America! America! God shed his grace on thee
And crown thy good with brotherhood
From sea to shining sea!
Amen

MIRACLES

¹ Therefore we must pay much closer attention to what we have heard, lest we drift away from it. ² For since the message declared by angels proved to be reliable, and every transgression or disobedience received a just retribution, ³ how shall we escape if we neglect such a great salvation? It was declared at first by the Lord, and it was attested to us by those who heard, ⁴ while God also bore witness by signs and wonders and various miracles and by gifts of the Holy Spirit distributed according to his will.

Hebrews 2: 1-4

Webster's dictionary: a miracle is a supernatural event regarded as due to divine action.

It is within this indelible work of the Spirit in the lives of the saints that some have been selected to be miracle bearers. Yes, we still have miracles within our midst!

The reality of present miracles is readily observable through the eyes of faith. The miracles are within our present circles of friends and acquaintances. When we observe a miracle, we need to stop and ask "why". The answer is always the same, "so that you may believe".

My friend Leah was given months or less to live after her diagnosis of stage 4 endometrial cancer. That original diagnosis was three and one-half years ago. Leah is a miracle! She not only has a will to live but also has a will to serve. She said recently "I wonder what God has in store for me to do"?

The question one seldom hears is that "does God still do miracles"? We all know the answer to be absolutely "yes". If that is our response, then why are we so reticent to be vocal about the miracles around us? Could it be that we don't want to call a miracle for what it is just in case there might be a reversal of symptoms? Yes, we all will readily admit to the absolute certainty of death and taxes but we're not so sure about calling a miracle for what it so apparently is. Why not celebrate the miracles around us? Yes, the cancers in remission, the shrinking tumors, the person who was given 24 months to live but lived symptom free for 22 years (my first wife).

On a conversational level, we speak glowingly about a hole in one, a great catch of fish, the exciting winning touchdown but why do we not speak of the miracles around us? Of all the conversations for us to have the topic of miracles past and present are "stepping-stones" to the mandated conversations that Jesus directed us to have just as he was about to ascend into heaven from his three-year ministry on earth. In Jesus words, "you'll receive power when the Holy Spirit has come upon you, and you'll be my witnesses in Jerusalem, and in all of Judea, Samaria and to the end of the earth". Acts 1:8

Prayer: Father, you have surrounded me with miracle healings, changed lives and people who will not call a miracle "a miracle" because it can't be scientifically explained. Give me the courage to open the conversational door that leads them to you. Amen

MOTORS

[1] Let brotherly love continue. [2] Do not neglect to show hospitality to strangers, for thereby some have entertained angels unawares.

Hebrews 13:1-2

Calvin College, now University, in the 1950's, my future wife and I were babysitting two precious little girls under four years of age. After being put to bed, the youngest started to cry after only being in her bed for less than fifteen minutes. We both inquired "what's wrong"? Her response was "there's a mosquito in my room". We said, "how do you know, it's too dark in your room to see a mosquito." Her response has been often quoted, "I know he's here; I can hear his motor running."

By observation, we draw conclusions from our senses which aren't always accurate. Body size, dress, cleanliness etc. we reach conclusions as to what position they might have in life such as couch potato, runner, laborer, business executive etc.

Sensing is one of our gifts from God so that we can assess our environment. Factors to consider are personal safety in certain neighborhoods, comfortable appealing restaurants that "catch our eye" etc.

The mosquito was very present. Its motor was permanently shut off and our cute little gal was soon off to dreamland without noisy motors.

Our internal sensing capabilities are similar to an internal GPS and sonar like perceptions. These capacities allow us to evaluate personal safety in certain environments. The ability to perceive what might lie ahead is a fabulous tool to guard us upon life's journey.

In addition, based upon our past experiences and those or our circle of friends, we attempt to assess new acquaintances by sheer observation and either "write them off" or "give them a chance".

Speaking personally, I've been far too quick to make snap assessments when meeting new people. In some cases, I blush with shame for being so far off the mark. I didn't really give the new person(s) a chance. Summed up, I didn't give them a chance to "hear their motor running".

James 1:19 fits perfectly: *Know this my beloved bothers: let every person be quick to hear, slow to speak, slow to anger.*

Prayer: Father, give me a sensitive sense of fellow image bearers. I want to hear and sense their "running motors". Amen

NO EXCUSES

¹The heavens declare the glory of God,
and the sky above proclaims his handiwork.
² Day to day pours out speech,
and night to night reveals knowledge.
³ There is no speech, nor are there words,
whose voice is not heard.
⁴ Their voice goes out through all the earth,
and their words to the end of the world.
In them he has set a tent for the sun,
⁵   which comes out like a bridegroom leaving his
chamber,
and, like a strong man, runs its course with joy.
⁶ Its rising is from the end of the heavens,
and its circuit to the end of them,
and there is nothing hidden from its heat.
Psalm 19: 1-6

Consider yourself in the largest symphony hall in all the world with literally over 100 plus musicians in the orchestra. A choir of two to three hundred singers are there to complete the sound. From the opening downbeat of the director's baton, be prepared to be "blown away" by the magnificence of the sound. The heavens on a daily basis exceed even the most excellent musical experience you could ever imagine.

My wife likes to describe changing cloud formations. Her vivid imagination sees all kinds of figures in the clouds. She truly is a fan of God's creation.

129

The heavens depict the universal speech available to all of mankind. What a shame that so many of us just take the excellence of nature for granted.

What an opportunity to enter into a discussion with others about the assurance of eternity by beginning the conversation with" this is the day the Lord has made, let us rejoice and be glad in it". Ps. 118:24. My old friend Dave from Promise Keepers times referred to this verse from Psalm 118 and it left an impression upon my mind.

Wayne, my former hunting and fishing friend from Traverse City, who now calls Heaven home, and I made a weeklong trip to the Missoula, Montana area in search of rainbow trout. What struck me is that once we entered the majestic mountains Wayne started to whisper. He was overwhelmed with the majesty of creation. Yes, we also found rainbow trout in abundance that we promptly sent back to the Bitterroot River after enjoying their acrobatic antics at the ends of our fly-rods.

When surrounded with the majesty of God's creation, it is logical to conclude that man has no excuse for denying the existence of a God who created all this beauty. The Apostle Paul sums it all up in Romans 1:20

[20] *For his invisible attributes, namely, his eternal power and divine nature, have been clearly perceived, ever since the creation of the world, in the things that have been made. So they are without excuse.*

Prayer: We see you in nature. Your creation is mind-blowing. May we rejoice in your work by our words and actions. Amen

PARABLES

Isaiah's Commission from the Lord:

[8] And I heard the voice of the Lord saying, "Whom shall I send, and who will go for us?" Then I said, "Here I am! Send me." [9] And he said, "Go, and say to this people:
"'Keep on hearing, but do not understand;
keep on seeing, but do not perceive.'
[10] Make the heart of this people dull,
and their ears heavy,
and blind their eyes;
lest they see with their eyes,
and hear with their ears,
and understand with their hearts,
and turn and be healed."
Isaiah 6: 8-10

[10] And when he was alone, those around him with the twelve asked him about the parables. [11] And he said to them, "To you has been given the secret of the kingdom of God, but for those outside everything is in parables, [12] so that they may indeed see but not perceive, and may indeed hear but not understand, lest they turn and be forgiven."
Mark 4:10-12

Jesus, a master teacher, was remembered in three of the four gospels with an explanation of why the use of parables. Each gospel speaks to why Jesus used parables to explain his lessons to others. Just the fact that three gospels explained the use of parables is a statement which speaks to the importance of their use. Jesus' explanation is recorded in three gospels using almost identical language. Also, the similarity of Jesus' words to Isaiah's commission from the Lord underscores the importance of communicating clearly and effectively with the most important lessons of the gospel.

In my personal experience as a freshman high school student, I was assigned to take plane geometry as a core course. Math was not a strong suit for me. My past experience was that I had to dig explanations out of a textbook for algebra and let's just say that math was not one of my favorite subjects. My dread of the geometry class was totally unnecessary. My teacher, George Johnson, was a weekend National Guard helicopter pilot. He explained the angles and diagrams of geometry from 5,000 feet altitude and now I could visualize very readily the geometrical problems. Thanks to Mr. Johnson, geometry became alive for me because my teacher was speaking to me using parables and illustrations that I could visualize.

Part of my vocational experience as an elementary principal was to evaluate teachers as they were teaching. Without a doubt, the teachers that resonated with the children and were the most successful, were those that made liberal use of illustrations. They were using the parable method.

Back to Jesus, the master teacher. Jesus utilized parables so that the listeners could visualize and understand and remember. Needless to say, we need pastors and educators to make liberal use of illustrations and word pictures to make their teaching come alive.

Our lesson from Jesus is that we are his communicators. It is our job to let others know by our actions and words what the gospel is all about. So many of us have great attendance records at church services and Sunday School classes. However, hcad knowledge is just part of being a Christian. We need to communicate the gospel story in our actions and our speech. We are part of a team that is out on the front lines representing Jesus. Our presence might be the only way others might see Jesus. Our peers look to us to see what Christianity looks like. Now's the time for parables and illustrations.

Prayer: Father, forgive the times that I didn't represent you adequately when I had the opportunity. Give me a sensitivity to see others as possibly needing my witness. Also, help me to use illustrations that are meaningful and interesting for your kingdom. Amen

PARENTING

*¹² As she continued praying before the LORD,
Eli observed her mouth.
¹³ Hannah was speaking in her heart; only her lips
moved, and her voice was not heard. Therefore Eli
took her to be a drunken woman.
¹⁴ And Eli said to her, "How long will you go on being
drunk? Put your wine away from you."
¹⁵ But Hannah answered, "No, my lord, I am a woman
troubled in spirit. I have drunk neither wine nor
strong drink, but I have been pouring out my soul
before the LORD.
¹⁶ Do not regard your servant as a worthless woman,
for all along I have been speaking out of my great
anxiety and vexation."
¹⁷ Then Eli answered, "Go in peace, and the God of
Israel grant your petition that you have made to him."
¹⁸ And she said, "Let your servant find favor in your
eyes." Then the woman went her way and ate, and
her face was no longer sad.*
I Samuel 1: 12-18

Hannah goes to God with her very fervent request for a
male child. She promises God that if he honors her
request, she will lend the child to the Lord. God honors
Hannah's request and she turns Samuel over to Eli for
mentoring and to later perform priestly duties for the rest
of his life. As an aside, God further honored this devoted
mother with other children after Samuel. Three sons and
two daughters followed.

Back to Eli. He rebukes his wayward sons who were making a mockery out of their temple duties. They carried on illicit affairs with whoever was available. In addition, they profaned the peace offerings that were brought to the temple. They kept an inordinate amount of the offerings for their own personal consumption.

Eli reprimands his sons because temple worshipers reported back to Eli that his sons were out of control. Eli offers the following rebuke to his sons:

> [22] *Now Eli was very old, and he kept hearing that his sons were doing to all Israel, and how they lay with women who were serving at the entrance to the tent of meeting.*
> [23] *And he said to them, "why do you do such things? For I hear of your evil dealings from all these people.*
> [24] *No, my sons, it is no good report that I hear from the people of the Lord spreading abroad.*
> [25] *If someone sins against a man, God will mediate for him but if someone sins against the Lord, who can intercede for him? "But they would not listen to the voice of their father, for it was the will of the Lord to put them to death.*
> *I Samuel 2: 22-25*

God took the lives of Eli and his two sons in one day. The sons were killed in battle and Eli upon hearing the news fell over backwards and broke his neck.

We really do not have a clear scriptural explanation of how Hannah and Eli exhibited different parenting styles. It is very apparent that Eli was a very liberal parent whose sons were allowed to profane the temple with their outrageous behavior. Apparently, Eli had to be told by others that his sons were involved in very sinful practices. Eli should have intervened when his sons were in their formative years.

Conversely, Hannah and her family lived a godly life and God blessed her with a large family after her giving Samuel to the lord.

In our society, parenting is tough. Two incomes are the norm to maintain a standard of living that is quite necessary. The children are involved in sports at school and, are expected to be on various travel teams. Family meals are a thing of the past for the most part.

Parenting is difficult to say the least. Involve them with you in church attendance, be aware of what they are studying in school especially in public schools. Much of the curriculum has been very left leaning and anti-scriptural. Your solutions are to have knowledge and if you don't approve, attend board meetings. If communication with the board doesn't work you have charter, private, home and Christian schools as an option. You only have your children in the formative years for a very short time. Treat your parenting with prayer.

Prayer: Father, we are often confused with how to properly raise our children. May Hannah's example speak to us. Amen.

RELATIONSHIPS

¹⁸ Then the Lord God said, "It is not good that the man should be alone; I will make a helper fit for him."
¹⁹ Now out of the ground the Lord had formed every beast of the field and every bird of the heavens and bought them to man to see what he would call them. And whatever the man had called every living creature, that was its name.
²⁰ The man gave names to all livestock and to the birds of the heavens and to every beast of the field. But for Adam there was not found a helper fit for him.
²¹ So the Lord God caused a deep sleep to fall upon the man, and while he slept took one of his ribs and closed up its place with flesh.
²² And the rib that the Lord God had taken from the man he made her into a woman and brought her to the man.
²³ Then the man said," This at last is bone of my bones and flesh of my flesh; she shall be called Woman, because she was taken out of man."
²⁴ Therefore, a man shall leave his father and his mother and hold fast to his wife, and they shall become one flesh.
Genesis 2:18-24

God said that it was not good for man to be alone, so God made the first woman out of the flesh of the first man. Truly this was bone from bone and flesh from flesh. This was the first marriage, and it was truly not only arranged but it was made by God

Physical and caring relationships were initiated by God. Since this originally pure relationship started between Adam and Eve then sin entered into the world. At this moment of sin, the relationship with God changed as did the relationship between the newlyweds.

However, God was already planning ahead and said that the deliverance from sin would arrive in the person of his son Jesus Christ on the cross.

At the advent of sin, man's thinking was drastically altered. Man saw the world through the eyes of sin and at the same time man, because he was created in the image of God, he was capable of having loving relationships.

With the arrival of sin, the symptoms of sin also arrived. It didn't take long for the first homicide to occur, born out of sinful jealousy. God, being a holy God could not coexist with evil and so Cain was given a protective mark and sent away into the land of Nod.

Since those early days of being sent to the world's best garden, man has been plagued with all sorts of maladies, illness, strife, relationship deterioration, financial downturns, death etc.

The question is why does God inflict upon his image bearers such difficulties and trials? The obvious answer is that God wants to get our attention away from ourselves and to worship him. Some of us when faced with trials, purposely attempt to "get back at God". We have a mindset that that if God really loved us why would he allow such difficulties to enter our lives. Really? Since when have you become the director of the actions of a holy God? God wants you to come to him in worship and praise not in worship that lacks your heart and devotion.

If you can't get over what life has dealt you, God hasn't moved but you have. Now is a time to internally reconcile yourself to God and to come back to him.

David's story is a classic example of one who sinned by committing adultery and an arranged murder. God punished him by taking the lives of his sons. Yet David comes to God with a contrite heart in Psalm 51. If you need to ask forgiveness because of your negative attitude toward God, read Psalm 51 with special emphasis on verses 10 and 11. These verses are our closing prayer.

Create in me a clean heart, O God, and renew a right spirit within me. Cast me not away from your presence and take not your Holy Spirit from me. Amen

SENIOR MINISTRY

¹ Do not rebuke an older man but encourage him as you would a father, younger men as brothers,
² older women as mothers, younger women as sisters, in all purity.
³ Honor the widows who are truly widows.
⁴ But if a widow has children or grandchildren, let them first learn to show godliness to their own household and to make some return to their parents, for this is pleasing in the sight of God.
⁵ She who is truly a widow, left all alone, and has set her hope on God and continues in supplications and prayers night and day,
⁶ but she who is self-indulgent is dead even while she lives.
⁷ Command these things as well, so that they may be without reproach.
⁸ But if anyone does not provide for his relatives, and especially for members of his household, he has denied the faith and is worse than an unbeliever.
I Timothy 5:1-8

Paul writes to his spiritual son, Timothy. He issues some fatherly advice about how a church should be sensitive to the needs of their senior citizens. This group of retirees are often overlooked and because we know something about them, we assume that their needs are all being met.

As an aside, Timothy was not a church pastor at Ephesus. He was a church leader who relied heavily upon Paul's mentorship. Paul's letter to Timothy takes place when the church at Ephesus is being plagued with many false teachers.

Currently, in this day of self-sufficiency, we can learn from Paul's insight into the possible needs of the church's seniors.

In today's society there is an assumption that because we have a general idea of a senior's situation on a spiritual, financial and physical level that we think their needs are being met. Paul in his letter to Timothy, is basically saying, "don't assume you know about your seniors just because you see them in worship.

If the senior has family ties available to them let the family meet the needs of their grandparents and parents.

However, to those seniors who are alone, the church needs to be "on top" of their needs. They need to know their needs on a physical, financial and spiritual level. Other seniors who do not have many needs are an excellent source of volunteers who can visit and call the seniors that are alone. Bear in mind that being alone is only one area of potential need. Some senior couples might just need some assistance too.

> Are there health needs?
> Do they need transportation to appointments and shopping?
> Does their property need repair?
> Are there cognition problems?
> Are they lonely and perhaps need a visit?
> Do they have an alert system?
> Is their neighborhood safe?

Perhaps you have some ideas as to what can be done in your church. Why not communicate with the church deacons and let them know.

Prayer: Father so often we overlook those in need because we aren't aware. Give us a sense of reaching out to those seniors that just might need someone to talk to or to offer to give them a ride etc. Amen

SIGNS

The blood shall be a sign for you, on the houses where
you are. And when I see the blood, I will pass over you,
and no plague will befall you to destroy you, when I
strike the land of Egypt.
Exodus 12:13

37 Now when they heard this they were cut to the
heart, and said to Peter and the rest of the apostles,
"Brothers, what shall we do?"
38 And Peter said to them, "Repent and be baptized
every one of you in the name of Jesus Christ for
the forgiveness of your sins, and you will receive
the gift of the Holy Spirit.
39 For the promise is for you and for your children
and for all who are far off, everyone whom the
Lord our God calls to himself."
Acts 2:37-39

We experience signs in our culture to the point of overkill. We have billboards, electronic billboards, traffic signs, business signs etc. We literally have so many signs that they take away from the raw beauty of the countryside.

Football and baseball would be a disaster without signs being exchanged between coaches and players. Referees and umpires communicate with known signs to communicate their decisions.

Even protests and parades carry signs to get their messages across to the crowds watching their parades.

Toward the end of Jesus' ministry, the Jews were asking for more signs from Jesus which was basically a stalling technique. The gospel had been clearly preached and instead of saying yes or no to the gospel, they hesitated and asked for more signs. They didn't need any additional signs. What they needed was to make a decision for Jesus.

The Greeks were more authentic. They were the students of the times. They truly wanted more wisdom.

The question really is the same for both Jews and Greeks, "what are you going to do with the gospel of Jesus?"

The Jewish tradition of celebrating the Passover is still being done. It is a major time of remembering the exodus from Egypt to the Promised Land but especially the blood of a lamb over the doorposts of each home.

We also have times of special celebrations remembering the birth of Jesus, his resurrection and the indwelling of the Holy Spirit. These are signs of the gospel and are more important than the other signs around us. These days of celebration are perfect times to invite a friend or a neighbor to worship with us and even to sit with us during worship.

In addition to all the signs and special days recorded in the Bible, there are many signs that take place in our own personal lives. Many of us have experienced miraculous healings, recovery from financial problems, recovery of our home life by improved conditions etc.

The overarching question is the same as was summarized in Peter's great Pentecost sermon, "repent and be baptized and you will receive the gift of the Holy Spirit."

Do you need more signs? No, it's decision time. What will you do with the plan of salvation? Regardless of your past, Jesus will forgive your confessed sins and accept you into his growing family. May God bless your decision.

Prayer: Father, forgive my sins of the past. I love you and will give you my best for the rest of my life. Amen

SLUGGARD

⁶ Go to the ant, O sluggard;
consider her ways, and be wise.
⁷ Without having any chief,
officer, or ruler,
⁸ she prepares her bread in summer
and gathers her food in harvest.
Proverbs 6: 6-8

An opening scene of my early education took place in a one room Christian grade school which housed grades 1-8. My desk was right next to the door which opened directly to the outside. It was a wood door with the upper one half composed of glass.

Our teacher was a middle-aged man who was slightly built but had a booming voice. One of the more unruly students (an eighth grader) angered our teacher/principal. Apparently, Clyde hadn't turned in his homework and was not about to get busy and complete his assignments. The teacher lost it and in his very loudest voice quoted directly from Proverbs and aimed directly at Clyde "go to the ant thou sluggard; consider her ways and be wise."

Clyde wasn't about to take the role of being a sluggard, so he ran to the exit door and slammed it with such force that my desk was littered with shattered window glass. This was quite a traumatic moment in the life of a shy five-year-old.

Even though at the time I had no idea what a sluggard was, I made a pact within myself to never become one. Now, decades later I can still recall the incident as if it were yesterday.

As each of us looks back upon our lives and the events that made an indelible mark upon us we probably can readily bring up events that have shaped us and caused us to think and shape our thinking. As Psalm 90:12 says, "so teach us to number our days that we may get a heart of wisdom." It appears that the incidents that we recall that shaped our behaviors and thinking were part of the process of numbering our days.

A simple definition of what it means to number our days is to pay attention to the various events of our lives that we have lived through and that God has watched over us. Think back how has God preserved your life and watched over you?

Prayer: Father you have brought us to this point in each one of our lives and we give you thanks for watching over us. You have given us opportunities to let others know how you are in charge of our days. We number them and give you all the glory. Amen

SPIKES UP

[11.] I saw that under the sun the race is not to the swift, nor the battle to the strong, nor bread to the wise, nor riches to the intelligent, nor favor to those with knowledge, but time and chance happen to them all.

[12.] For man does not know his time. Like fish are taken in an evil net, and like birds that are caught in a snare, so the children of man are snared at an evil time, when it suddenly falls upon them.
Ecclesiastes 9:11-12

We have no idea how God measures time. We do know however that he is unwavering in keeping his promises. The promises of God are absolutes. It all started in the Garden of Eden with Adam and Eve violating God's command and sure enough, God's judgement was immediate in that they were expelled from the garden to a life of sweaty toil and eventual mortal death.

Now we wait for the second coming of Jesus. At that time our present existence will end and we will be caught up to our eternal home with our resurrected bodies. We don't know when but we do know that it will happen absolutely on God's unpublished time schedule.

Every one of us who has raised a family is familiar with the rhetoric from the backseat, "are we there yet." As children we have an immature conception of time. We just can't wait for Christmas, our birthday, school to end, school to start etc.

During our adult life, it seems like the years are going by faster. Before we know it, our kids ae raised and we are "empty nesters". Life has gone by in a blur.

It is during this latter part of our working years that we become more aware of our mortality. We take more seriously the words of Psalm 90 which speaks of our life spans.

[10] The years of our lives are seventy, or even by reason of strength eighty; yet their span is but toil and trouble; they are soon gone, and we fly away.
[12] So teach us to number our days that we may get a heart of wisdom

Our retirement finally comes, and we start emptying our bucket list of the things we have been putting off. We travel, maybe volunteer, spend more time with the grandchildren, and in general we attempt to give back in other creative ways.

When you enter the last chapter of your life, may you have the assurance that heaven will be your final destination. A friend of mine knew that his days were numbered in single digits and he has since passed on into glory. We tried to visit him over our traditional annual lunch, but Dick wasn't up to it. His wife said maybe a desert might be fine with a cup of joe. So three old buddies delivered cherry pie which was "just right" for our friend. Before we could even finish the "small talk" Dick said, "I want you guys to stop praying for my healing. I'm coming around third and I'm beginning my slide home and I'm coming in "spikes up". So don't, don't block the plate.

That is the positive assurance that we all need to have when we round third. Where are you at with Jesus? He is standing at the plate and is waiting.

Prayer: Lord may we utilize your time which you have allocated for us with a positive hope for salvation. Amen

STRESS

Stress is probably one of the leading factors that affects our mental and physical lives. It is present in each one of our lives. It is perceived by each individual in their own unique way.

Some of us experience stress that is job related. This can be caused by demanding management, negative working conditions as shown by fellow workers that are negative about most job-related conditions. Solutions to stress might be to meet with management one on one and seek reasons and/or changes.

Marital stress is very difficult to deal with. Solutions might begin with honest in-depth conversations between spouses. Sometimes entire families need to sit down and "clear the air". The sources of stress are endless. In fact, many experience stress and are totally oblivious to it being present.

As an aside, we as Christians need to be sensitive to the needs of others that may be overwhelmed with stress. We just might observe one of our friends acting out in an "over the top" manner. This behavior could be stress related. This might be an opportunity to meet for a cup of coffee and a friendly conversation.

This past Labor Day was a wonderful time of meeting with my extended family around a backyard pool. Good conversation sprinkled the day, and one topic was that of stress. We all agreed that stress was present in all of our lives and that people deal with stress in a multitude of ways. Some receive medication, others medicate themselves and some exercise or watch television or read. My grandson, a medical doctor concluded the conversation with a quotation take from Matthew 6. He stated that when followed, it is the only real cure for the handling of stress. We all agreed. My unanswered question is why isn't the cure for stress the first solution that we reach out to? Perhaps this observation might be a good topic for you and your friends and/or family to discuss.

> *25 Therefore, I tell you, do not be anxious about your life, what you will eat or what you will drink, nor about your body, what you will put on. Is not life more than food, and the body more than clothing?*
> *26 Look at the birds of the air: they neither sow nor reap nor gather into barns, and yet your heavenly Father feeds them, are you not of more value than they?*
> *27 And which of you by being anxious can add a single hour to his span of life?*
> *28 Why are you anxious about clothing? Consider the lilies of the field, how they grow: they neither toil nor spin,*
> *29 Yet I tell you, even Solomon in all his glory was not arrayed like one of these.*
> *30 But if God so clothes the grass of the field, which today is alive and tomorrow is thrown into the oven, will he not much more clothe you, O you of little faith?*

^{31} Therefore do not be anxious, saying, "What shall we eat"? Or "what shall drink?" or "What shall we wear?"
^{32} For the Gentiles seek after all these things, and your heavenly Father knows that you need them all.
^{33} But seek first the kingdom of God and his righteousness, and all these things will be added to you.
^{34} Therefore do not be anxious about tomorrow, for tomorrow will be anxious for itself. Sufficient for the day is its own trouble.

Matthew 6:25-34

Prayer:

Father, we all have situations in our lives that give us anxiety. We ask that your promises of divine care will give us a peace from our cares. Amen

THE PURPOSE OF THE PARABLES

10 Then the disciples came and said to him, "Why do you speak to them in parables?" 11 And he answered them, "To you it has been given to know the secrets of the kingdom of heaven, but to them it has not been given. 12 For to the one who has, more will be given, and he will have an abundance, but from the one who has not, even what he has will be taken away. 13 This is why I speak to them in parables, because seeing they do not see, and hearing they do not hear, nor do they understand. 14 Indeed, in their case the prophecy of Isaiah is fulfilled that says:

'"You will indeed hear but never understand,
and you will indeed see but never perceive."
15 For this people's heart has grown dull,
and with their ears they can barely hear,
and their eyes they have closed,
lest they should see with their eyes
and hear with their ears
and understand with their heart
and turn, and I would heal them.'

Matthew 13: 10-15

In my time spent as an elementary principal, it was my pleasure to observe the different teaching styles of various teachers. Some styles were very much in step with textbooks and study guides where all the students were expected to all be "on the same page". However, one of my more successful teachers began to individualize her approach to teaching in that she met each child where they were at and then taught them in their comfort and understanding zone. Wow, the difference was soon noticed by other teachers and they too began to individualize their teaching methods.

Jesus utilized parables to enhance understanding. When the disciples questioned his use of parables, Jesus basically said that illustrations were necessary to enhance understanding. The use of parables was recorded in three of the gospels thus giving emphasis to the attraction of their use in connecting with the people. Also, Jesus was followed by crowds of people. Without a doubt they were in love with this teacher that healed and spoke in a language that met them where they were.

For those of us in the communication areas of education and church ministry, we can learn from Jesus the master teacher. Churches that are attracting increasing numbers of members are those that preach the Word of God in clarity and truth. Schools that have great reputations in the community are the ones that stick to the basics.

When we think back over the years of our favorite preachers and memorable teachers, I believe that we remember best those that used illustrations (parables). What a lesson for all of us who want to connect with others.

The main point of this meditation is that as followers of Jesus, we have a message of salvation to impart to those people that we interact with. Now it's time to be intentional in getting our message across. It is time to use some illustrations. (parables)

Prayer: Father, when the Spirit nudges me to share your gospel, give me clarity of thought and illustrations that will speak to hearts. Amen

TIME TO THINK

Finally, brothers, whatever is true, whatever is honorable, whatever is just, whatever is pure, whatever is lovely, whatever is commendable, if there is any excellence, if there is anything worthy of praise, think about these things.

Philippians 4:8

When do you have time to think in depth? Our society is driven to seek out things that perform for us at faster paces than what we presently work with and enjoy. Some items become obsolete especially in the arena of technology and we are motivated to invest in items that perform tasks more efficiently and in less time.

Demand is created for:

1. Faster internet
2. TV streaming with or without ads
3. Cars that almost drive for us.
4. Remote control of our electrical appliances

The list goes on and on. Recently, over dinner with a grandson and his wife, he posed a question "what are you doing for your devotional time? Great question for a fast-paced society. I suspect that many of us have abbreviated times to get alone with our thoughts and with God. I know that my personal time of devotional thinking has peaks and valleys. When life is smooth, my meditation time suffers. When difficulties come my way, my devotional life deepens and gets more focused.

How about right now. Take a brief "time out" to ask yourself the question if you're taking the time to think about what is honorable, just, pure, lovely, commendable, excellence, worthy of praise.

Think about these things.

Prayer:

Father, forgive my abbreviated and or missing times that I'm spending in your word and prayer. Teach me the lesson of being content with where I'm at right now. Amen

TRACKING

[14] Bless those who persecute you; bless and do not curse them. [15] Rejoice with those who rejoice, weep with those who weep. [16] Live in harmony with one another. Do not be haughty, but associate with the lowly. Never be wise in your own sight. [17] Repay no one evil for evil, but give thought to do what is honorable in the sight of all. [18] If possible, so far as it depends on you, live peaceably with all. [19] Beloved, never avenge yourselves, but leave it to the wrath of God, for it is written, "Vengeance is mine, I will repay, says the Lord." [20] To the contrary, "if your enemy is hungry, feed him; if he is thirsty, give him something to drink; for by so doing you will heap burning coals on his head." [21] Do not be overcome by evil, but overcome evil with good.
Romans 12:14-21

Hunting with my son and his sons is a high point of my role as a father and grandfather. Hunting consists of picking a likely spot for game to appear. However, tracking is the key to find that best spot for deer to visit. Veteran hunters can "read" the signs of deer movement and habits. Hunters who are very successful track their game prior to the onset of the hunting season and are prepared to wait for the deer to appear on opening day.

In the above scripture we are given all kinds of advice on how to interact. Our actions are to "track" others in a way that is sensitive to their needs. So there is a time to weep and a time to laugh. In so doing, we can empathize with others and show our love and witness. So when you are "tracking" others you are being sensitive. You "are there for them". "You have their back". Never should you gossip to others the confidences shared during your times of consoling hurting people. Instead, you sit with them, you listen without sharing the woes of others including those of your own. Listening is the key to spiritual tracking. Only by your presence can we really listen. Cards, texts and e-mails are better than no contact but your presence, your listening, and your empathy is the ultimate way to "being there for them".

The next level of "tracking" is to "bend over backwards for the "hard to love". These are the people that have lost their smile years ago. They are judgmental and demanding. So now is the time to "heap burning coals on their heads". All we can do is love them to the best of our capabilities and leave the judgmental decisions up to God.

This "tracking" of others in need isn't easy. In fact, many times it causes us great internal discomfort. However, many times that we dread are often turned into times of internal blessing when we "were there" for the hard to love person.

Prayer: Father, forgive me and my judgmental mind and give me a loving heart that reaches out to others that need you through me and my loving visit. Amen

UNDER CONSTRUCTION

[10] According to the grace of God given to me, like a skilled master builder I laid a foundation, and someone else is building upon it. Let each one take care how he builds upon it.
[11] For no one can lay a foundation other than that which is laid, which is Jesus Christ.
[12] Now if anyone builds on the foundation with gold, silver, precious stones, wood, hay, straw—
[13] each one's work will become manifest, for the Day will disclose it, because it will be revealed by fire, and the fire will test what sort of work each one has done.
[14] If the work that anyone has built on the foundation survives, he will receive a reward.
[15] If anyone's work is burned up, he will suffer loss, though he himself will be saved, but only as through fire.
[16] Do you not know that you are God's temple and that God's Spirit dwells in you?
[17] If anyone destroys God's temple, God will destroy him. For God's temple is holy, and you are that temple.
I Corinthians 3: 10-17

Being a bachelor at age 74 was a unique experience for me. My wife of 54 blessed years went on to her eternal reward of glory. After about three months of keeping myself busy with interior painting of my home, my daughter gave me some sage advice: "Dad why don't you do some woodworking. When my boys were younger, they spent hours on the rocking horse that you built?" So

I proceeded to outfit a workshop in the unfinished basement of my home.

A good friend, who had much more experience in working with wood became my mentor, my close friend, more accurately my soul mate. We even finished a dining room table for my daughter in law. It only took three years of laughter, marginal language and finally some exclamations of approval. Table completed!

Spiritually, we are all examples of what our lives should look like under construction. When we adhere to God's Word for our lives, things go along much more smoothly.

The Apostle Paul in today's scripture gives a wonderful example of what our earthly temples (bodies) should look like. If you are able, align yourself with a soul mate with whom you can confidentially share your thoughts, doubts, hopes, goals, failures etc. We are all "under construction" and the temple in which you reside needs to be measured, sized, planed, sawn and appraised by another set of eyes and ears. (Your soul mate)

The table is now completed. However, the temple is still under construction and needs some constructive changes. How's your temple going? You are a holy creation and God lives within you. Your family and peers are observing and listening.

Prayer: Father, today I'm evaluating my temple. It's not perfect. I ask for your Spirit to work within me and plane me to be a sharper temple image. Amen

WEDDING AT CANA

On the third day there was a wedding at Cana in Galilee, and the mother of Jesus was there. [2] Jesus was also invited to the wedding with his disciples. [3] When the wine ran out, the mother of Jesus said to him, "They have no wine." [4] And Jesus said to her, "Woman, what does this have to do with me? My hour has not yet come." His mother said to the servants, "Do whatever he tells you." [6] Now there were six stone jars there for the Jewish rites of purification, each holding twenty or thirty gallons. [7] Jesus said to the servants, "Fill the jars with water." And they filled them up to the brim. [8] And he said to them, "Now draw some out and take it to the master of the feast." So they took it. [9] When the master of the feast tasted the water now become wine, and did not know where it came from (though the servants who had drawn the water knew), the master of the feast called the bridegroom [10] And said to him, "Everyone serves the good wine first, and when the people have drunk freely, then the poor wine. But you have kept the good wine until now." [11] This, the first of his signs, Jesus did at Cana in Galilee, and manifested his glory. And his disciples believed in him.

John 2: 1-11

Shortly after Jesus had called his disciples, we see all of them including Jesus' mother at a wedding in Cana. Jesus had just invited Nathanael to be a disciple. Nathanael became convinced of Jesus authenticity when Jesus said that he knew about Nathanael's whereabouts even before the two had met. Nathanael immediately proclaimed his belief in Jesus as being the Messiah.

At the wedding, we find Jesus together with the disciples and Jesus' mother attending. Wine was generally served at weddings in that it was a symbol of God's blessing. When the wine supply ran out, Jesus' mother notifies Jesus of the fact. Jesus addresses his mother as "Woman" which was a term of social distancing. Jesus explains that his hour of trial and crucifixion is quite distant. At this time of Jesus' ministry, he is placing emphasis on individuals privately instead of concentrating on the general public.

The miracle of changing 120 plus gallons of water into fine wine was done for a specific reason. It was the first of seven signs in the gospel of John to point specifically to Jesus as the Messiah.

For Jesus to be recognized as the Messiah was absolutely essential as a cornerstone of Jesus' ministry and the plan of salvation. In a way, this first miracle was basically Jesus' "coming out party". Just imagine the conversations among the guests wondering where this fine wine had come from. Also, just who is this Jesus?

A lesson for all of us lies in our interactions with others. None of us will attend a wedding with Jesus as a guest until the great wedding feast of the Lamb in heaven. However, as we mix with people, we just might be the only likeness of Jesus in the room.

How will we conduct ourselves? It seems that we have two choices. One choice is to do everything to blend in with the group and participate in all their secular speech and actions. Doing so, we will compromise all possibilities of a Christian witness.

Another choice is to be friends with as many as possible but to look for opportunities to let our surrounding peoples know that Jesus lives within us. Simply put, we might not ever have another time to let others know that we are believers. Jesus brought wine to the celebration to draw attention to his role as the Messiah. We bring ourselves and we bring Jesus. Are you up to it?

Prayer: Father as we associate with others, may we represent you with elegance and earnestness. Help us to be faithful witnesses. Amen

WEEDS

He put another parable before them, saying, " The kingdom of heaven may be compared to a man who sowed good seed in his field, [25] *but while his men were sleeping, his enemy came and sowed weeds among the wheat and went away.* [26] *So when the plants came up and bore grain, then the weeds appeared also.* [27] *And the servants of the master of the house came and said to him, "Master did you not sow good seed in your field? How then does it have weeds?"* [28] *He said to them, "An enemy has done this." So the servants said to him, "Then do you want us to go and gather them?* [29] *But he said, "No, lest in gathering the weeds you root up the wheat along with them.* [30] *Let both grow together until the harvest, and at harvest time I will tell the reapers, "Gather the weeds first and bind them in bundles to be burned, but gather the wheat into my barn."*
Matthew 13: 24-30

Weeds are my nemesis for not using a weed screen material after preparing a flower garden area. Many hours are spent pulling weeds and later in desperation, I apply a herbicide.

Today's parable pictures someone who was out to spoil the farmer's wheat crop. The vindictive spoiler of the wheat field probably planted darnel among the wheat. Darnel is a weedy rye that closely resembles wheat but at maturity bears small poisonous seeds.

We don't know the dynamics of what motivated someone to undermine the wheat crop. The scripture doesn't share the reason for the attempted spoiling of the wheat crop. My speculative guess is that the spoiler was probably jealous of the farmer who planted the wheat.

The wheat and the weeds were allowed to grow together because to eradicate the weeds prior to wheat harvest would do extensive damage to the wheat crop.

In our world God allows believers to mingle with unbelievers. Many sects have been formed to isolate themselves from others who do not share their belief system. Let's face it, when you isolate yourself from others who do not share your beliefs, life is much less challenging. However, one does not thrive spiritually when one is surrounded by only those that share your belief system. Christians who mix their time with unbelievers are automatically being salt and light to others. Needless to say when one interacts with non-believers, it is an opportunity to be obedient to the great commission.

Weed pulling and weed eradication has taken on a new meaning. Where are you at in your spiritual gardening?

Prayer: Father give me the desire to go and actively seek out others that could profit from my spiritual gardening methods. Amen

WHERE ARE YOU COMING FROM?

¹⁰ Then Moses and Aaron gathered the assembly together before the rock, and he said to them, "Hear now, you rebels: shall we bring water for you out of this rock?"
¹¹ And Moses lifted up his hand and struck the rock with his staff twice, and water came out abundantly, and the congregation drank, and their livestock.
¹² And the LORD said to Moses and Aaron, "Because you did not believe in me, to uphold me as holy in the eyes of the people of Israel, therefore you shall not bring this assembly into the land that I have given them."
¹³ These are the waters of Meribah, where the people of Israel quarreled with the LORD, and through them he showed himself holy.
Numbers 20: 10-13

Moses is one of the great saints of all time. Yet Moses had an attitude problem at Meribah. He showed his attitude of anger toward the Israelites in addressing them as rebels and then he hit the rock twice with his staff. Yes, water came out and the people had plenty for themselves and their livestock, but God knew Moses inner anger and temporary unbelief. So God told Moses that he would not have the honor of leading the Israelites all the way into the promised land. Moses' assistant, Joshua would have the leadership role for the remainder of the exodus. God and Moses ascended Mt. Nebo and from the mountain elevation, God showed the promised land to Moses. Moses died on that mountain at the age of 120. God buried Moses in a spot that is unknown to man.

Moses had commissioned Joshua by laying on of hands previously. This example of passing on leadership is an example of excellent planning. It would take the strong leadership of Joshua to complete the exodus.

Another lesson is that Moses, in spite of his great leadership role that communed with God on a face-to-face basis, was a man afflicted with original sin and only God could "read his heart".

As you analyze your own internal motivation for all of your demeanor, are you acting out of a spirit of saying thanks to God for his great plan of salvation? God knows your soul – your motivation. He knows "where you are coming from."

Prayer: I want to live a thanks filled life, Father. May my reasoning be blessed by you. Amen

WHERE ARE YOU GOING?

¹ O LORD, you have searched me and known me!
² You know when I sit down and when I rise up;
you discern my thoughts from afar.
³ You search out my path and my lying down
and are acquainted with all my ways.
Psalm 139:1-3

²³ Search me, O God, and know my heart!
Try me and know my thoughts!
²⁴ And see if there be any grievous way in me,
and lead me in the way everlasting!
Psalm 139: 23-24

Fishing is one of my passions and is readily available in the area where I live because there are many lakes and rivers. It was one of my earliest exposures to fishing when I was about five years old. In an old wooden rowboat, on a small California irrigation reservoir, with my cousin, Ed and my dad. We didn't worry about safety precautions in those early days. I stood up in the boat to attempt to land a huge bluegill, lost my balance and fell overboard. The water was about 15 feet deep and because of my swimming ability I quickly surfaced, and Ed easily hoisted me back into the boat. I recall that my dad blurted out as I was falling in "where are you going Butch?" (my nickname used only by my dad at that time).

We just rented a boat, bought bait and rowed to a likely spot. By sharp contrast, we today are expected to have definable goals especially when being interviewed for another position or for a change in employer. A common question is "where do you wish to be in five years from now?"

A question that needs to be answered by everyone is "where are you going to spend eternity?" If you know for sure that you'll arrive in heaven after you die, then how are you spending your present days? Are you just waiting? Or are you living in joyous anticipation? Are you aware that Jesus has forgiven all your sins of the past, present and future? Yes Jesus died once for all the sins of everyone who is a Christian. When you consider the complete forgiveness brought about by Jesus on the cross, then doesn't it give you an absolute answer to the question we all face, "where are you going after you die?"

So where are you going? If you know that you'll be in heaven, let others know, just maybe you might be instrumental in answering the question that we all must answer "where are you going eternally?"

Prayer: Father, thank you for your saving grace that has forgiven all my sins of the past, present and future. I live in the assurance that my salvation is secure forever. Amen

WHY?

[7] *The end of all things is at hand; therefore be self-controlled and sober minded for the sake of your prayers.*

[8] *Above all, keep loving one another earnestly, since love covers a multitude of sins.*

[9] *Show hospitality to one another without grumbling.*

[10] *As each has received a gift, use it to serve one another, as good stewards of God's varied grace:*

[11] *whoever speaks, as one who speaks oracles of God; whoever serves, as one who serves by the strength that God supplies—in order that in everything God may be glorified through Jesus Christ. To him belong glory and dominion forever and ever. Amen.*

[12] *Beloved, do not be surprised at the fiery trial when it comes upon you to test you, as though something strange were happening to you.*

[13] *But rejoice insofar as you share Christ's sufferings, that you may also rejoice and be glad when his glory is revealed*

[14] *If you are insulted for the name of Christ, you are blessed, because the Spirit of glory[a] and of God rests upon you.*

[15] *But let none of you suffer as a murderer or a thief or an evildoer or as a meddler.*

[16] *Yet if anyone suffers as a Christian, let him not be ashamed, but let him glorify God in that name.*

[17] *For it is time for judgment to begin at the household of God; and if it begins with us, what will be the*

outcome for those who do not obey the gospel of God?
[18] And "If the righteous is scarcely saved,
what will become of the ungodly and the sinner?"
[19] Therefore let those who suffer according to God's
will entrust their souls to a faithful Creator while doing
good.
I Peter 4: 7-19

"Why" is an overused word by very young children, many of whom are precocious, wanting to know how things work and why some activities are prohibited etc.

New Christians typically need to know the "whys" to be answered that pertain to what Christianity is all about. What changes should take place in one's life by becoming a Christian? If I embrace Jesus Christ as my savior, will my family and friends be okay with the decision? Once all the "whys" have been answered, the new believer prays the "Sinner's Prayer" of confession and another new person has moved toward the eternal heavenly reward.

However, as most of us have experienced, negative happenings can and do take place in the lives of both Christians and non-Christians. It is only natural for a Christian to question how bad things can happen to a Christian. After all, is not the God I worship a God of love? The simple answer to one's question of "why" really has no mortal and logical answer. Sometimes our difficulties are self-inflicted by our lifestyles. Yet that is not the ultimate answer of "why" did my God allow this severe problem to enter into my life?

So how do Christians deal with the "whys" of life? The typical problems are the death of a child or a spouse. Marital strife is another common problem, financial problems, etc. Simply put, all of mankind faces problems that have no mortal explanation of "why" did it happen?

Some of the people react in many different ways to problems. Some are drawn closer to God in times of adversity. Their prayer lives and lifestyles becomes more God centered than was previously the case. Others draw into a cocoon type of existence and secretly blame God for allowing them to experience such a drastic turn of events. In fact such behavior, if continued for a long period of time can become a grudge against God.

The only reason that we mortals have that makes sense for our spiritual lives is that we seldom grow in our Christianity unless we are faced with problems that we can't solve readily or personally. Yes, a holy God allows bad things to happen to his children! Many times, God is trying to get our attention. Our rational mindset of asking "why" for a lifetime is our attempt to have God's actions be in accordance with our expectations. If God changed according to our wishes, he would cease to be God. However, prayer does modify our experiences, but it does not replace the holiness of God.

So what is the solution to our accepting the unsolvable negatives of life? Simply put, there is no one answer. The apostle Peter in his closing statement in verse 19 advises us to entrust our souls to our faithful Creator while doing good.

J.C. Watts pastor and politician sums up the thinking on how we handle the overwhelming "whys" of life. *"It doesn't take a lot of strength to hang on. It takes a lot of strength to let go."*

Prayer: Help us to not only let go, but to also let you become the main positive in our lives. Mold us and make us after your will. Amen

WORTHY

"Don't end your life wondering why you lived". This was stated by Dr. Tony Evans, founder and senior pastor of the 10,000-member Oak Cliff Bible Fellowship in Dallas.

Wondering about our worth should be a key question in each person's life. For today's consideration, the analysis of worth falls into the areas of financial worth, societal worth and spiritual worth.

When sitting down with a financial planner, the bottom-line topic is net worth. The factors utilized in arriving at the place of "where the rubber meets the road" of financial analysis are age, present income, future expected income, debt and retirement goals. The discussion will result in current net worth and will also render a projection of financial status into retirement years.

Coupled with the facts as developed by the financial analyst could be a state of complacency when one has filled his hypothetical barns to overflowing and is building others just in case. After all you might never know. Scripture speaks to this not uncommon mindset.

The land of a rich man produced plentifully, [17] and he thought to himself, "What shall I do, for I have nowhere to store my crops?" [18] And he said, "I will do this: I will tear down my barns and build larger ones, and there I

will store all my grain and my goods. ¹⁹ And I will say to
my soul, "Soul you have ample goods laid up for many
years; relax, eat, drink and be merry." ²⁰ But God said
to him, "Fool! This night your soul is required of you,
and the things you have prepared, whose will they be?"
²¹ So is the one who lays up treasure for himself and is
not rich toward God."
Luke 12:16b-21

Self-worth is also evaluated by our families and others in our circle of influence. Societal approval is a most cherished value for many of us. In fact, it often underlines our personal feelings of self-worth. A potential problem arises when acquired wealth places an individual on a pedestal of adoration. True humility is difficult when one is idolized primarily for their net worth.

Romans 3: 9-12 puts all of mankind in the same original category.

"None is righteous, no, not one; no one understands; no
one seeks for God.

¹² All have turned aside; together they have become
worthless; no one does good, not even one."

The apostle Paul, in his letter to the church at Thessalonica put things in perspective.

11 To this end we always pray for you, that our God
may make you worthy of his calling and may fulfill
every resolve for good and every work of faith by his
power, 12 so that the name of our Lord Jesus may be

glorified in you, and you in him according to the grace of our God and the Lord Jesus Christ.

II Thessalonians 1: 11-12

The end result of our calling is to have so lived that Jesus Christ is glorified by our words and total demeanor. The summations of our lives are for the glory of God and him alone.

Prayer: Father as I look within myself to ascertain my worthiness, it is only through your grace that I am considered worthy through the death and resurrection of your son Jesus Christ. May my future focus be on your kingdom and may my life reflect that worthiness by your grace. Amen

A Line in the Sand

And I pleaded with the Lord at that time, saying "O lord
God you have only begun to show your servant your
greatness and your mighty hand. For what god is there
in heaven or on earth who can do such works and
mighty acts as yours? Please let me go over and see the
good land beyond the Jordan, that good hill country and
Lebanon. "But the Lord was angry with me because of
you and would not listen to me. And the Lord said to me
"Enough from you; do not speak to me of this matter
again. Go up to the top of Pisgah and lift up your eyes
westward and northward and southward and eastward,
and look at it with your eyes, for you shall not go over
this Jordan. But charge Joshua, and encourage and
strengthen him, for he shall go over at the head of this
people, and he shall put them in possession of the land
that you shall see."
Deuteronomy 3:23-28

In our current political scene, there is a phrase that
is commonly used called "a line in the sand". Such a
phrase has been used as a deterrent to an enemy that has
or is "pushing our buttons" to ascertain how far we will
go to protect our country and past reputation as a world
power.

The scene is quite similar at the time of the exodus. The
Jews had been led by Moses with God supplying food in
the form of manna and quail. In addition, God's GPS in
the form of a cloud by day and fire by night gave
direction over the trailless desert sands. Yet the entire
exodus was marked by the whining Jews who at times

said that dying in Egypt was preferable to the physical challenges of the arid desert.

Moses pleaded with God to show mercy and allow the present generation to continue with Moses' leadership to cross into the Promised Land. God replied to Moses that the line had been crossed and there was to be no more discussion on the topic. God relented to a degree in allowing Moses to peek into the Holy land from the top of Mt. Pisgah.

In today's society, we would expect God to change His mind and allow Moses to continue based on good behavior. Yet the holiness of God is an absolute and the line had been crossed.

However, the exodus continues without the present generation of those who had left Egypt including Moses. Teach your children regarding their history and God's leadership. Tell them about the holy God who is loving and firm and absolute in all His decrees.

We too are engaged in a daily exodus on the way to eternity. Walk with God. Look for his leading in giving us our daily bread and spiritual leadership. So how are we to walk? A summation is beautifully stated in Micah 4:5b we will walk in the name of the Lord our God for ever and ever.

Prayer:
Father, forgive my times of going my own way and becoming negative when things didn't go my way. Lead me and change my heart to wait for your guidance. Amen

Abraham Tested

When they came to the place of which God had told him, Abraham built an altar there and laid the wood in order and bound Isaac his son and laid him on the altar, on top of the wood. Then Abraham reached out his hand and took the knife to slaughter his son. But the angel of the Lord called to him from heaven and said "Abraham, Abraham!" And he said "Here I am."
he said "Do not lay your hand on the boy or do anything to him for now I know that you fear God, seeing you have not withheld your son, your only son, from me."
And Abraham lifted up his eyes and looked, and behold, behind him was a ram, caught in a thicket by his horns. And Abraham went and took the ram and offered it up as a burnt offering instead of his son.
Genesis 22: 9-13

The most difficult scripture for me as a father is the account of Abraham's testing. Placing oneself in Abraham's shoes and wondering how one would respond is probably a primary reason the testing record of Abraham is recorded in the Bible.

Abraham needed to be tested for his own sake and the reinforcement of his spiritual self-confidence. God already knew the outcome in advance.

It is significant that Abraham took some servants along on the three day journey. Their presence provided moral support and gave veracity to the outcome of the testing.

Also, Abraham had three days to ponder his God given mandate.

Let's not forget Isaac. What a lesson for a budding young man. Just imagine the words of his father, "the Lord will provide" being forever etched into his memory bank. The entire sixth chapter of Deuteronomy gives directions of passing down to children and their children how God has led them throughout their existence. "The Lord will provide" is now added to that recollection of God's care and providential leadership.

The outcome of the testing shows an angel speaking to Abraham. The essence of the message is that Abraham is to be the "Father of a great nation". Therefore, he had to be tested with the ultimate test of allegiance to God's leading.

If you are in a difficult situation, perhaps God is testing you. Are you being groomed for some task yet unknown to you? It is only in the valleys of life that we grow spiritually. If you are being tested now, take comfort in the words, "the Lord will provide."

Prayer:
Father, as I look at my life, I see you. As others observe and listen to me, I pray that they will see you in me. Amen

Be Strong and Courageous

Be strong and courageous, for you shall cause this people to inherit the land that I swore to their fathers to give them. 7 Only be strong and very courageous, being careful to do according to all the law that Moses my servant commanded you. Do not turn from it to the right hand or to the left, that you may have good success wherever you go. 8 This book of the Law shall not depart from your mouth, but you shall meditate on it day and night, so that you may be careful to do according to all that is written in it. For then you will make your way prosperous, and then you will have good success. 9 Have I not commanded you? Be strong and courageous. Do not be frightened, and do not be dismayed, for the Lord your God is with you wherever you go.
Joshua 1:6-9

A phrase that resonates in my very viscera is the supportive statement of God to Joshua. "Be strong and courageous." At an annual Promise Keepers convention some years ago in Indianapolis, an "on fire" pastor, E. B. Hill, used the challenge of being "strong and courageous "to the near capacity attendance in the RCA Dome in Indianapolis.

In today's society of political correctness, the words of God "to be strong and courageous" would be labeled by non-believing pundits as being inappropriate and divisive.

Yet Joshua was specifically selected by God to be the successor of Moses and to continue and complete the exodus to the promised land. The land could not have become the property and home of the Israelites without armed conflict. Yes, armed conflict as authorized and directed by God and led by the strong and courageous, Joshua.

Each of us has a God ordained task. Some are selected to a specific vocation and others are used to be examples and ambassadors of the gospel on the assembly line, truck stop restaurant or wherever God has placed us.

We all have a calling. Not one of us is called to only make sure of our own calling and election and ignore the unsaved that surround us at work and wherever we are.

So as you enter your mission field "be strong and courageous". Joshua 1:5 states that no one will be able to stand up against you all the days of your life.

Prayer:
Lord make me strong and courageous as I interact with those that you direct to me . Amen

Blessed Assurance

5For this very reason, make every effort to supplement your faith with virtue, and virtue with knowledge 6 and knowledge with self-control, and self-control with steadfastness, and steadfastness with godliness, 7 and godliness with brotherly affection and brotherly affection with love.8 For if these qualities are yours and are increasing, they keep you from being ineffective or unfruitful in the knowledge of our Lord Jesus Christ. 9 For whoever lacks these qualities is so nearsighted that he is blind, having forgotten that he was cleansed from his former sins.10 Therefore, brothers, be all the more diligent to confirm your calling and election, for if you practice these qualities you will never fall.11 For in this way there will be richly provided for you an entrance into the eternal kingdom of our Lord and Savior Jesus Christ.
11Peter 1:5-11

Remember the old joke about a husband who never tells his wife that he loves her? His response to her question as to why was "I told you once and if I ever change my mind, I'll let you know".

Perhaps some of us have become lax in our response to God. It's so easy to fall into a rut of thinking that we're saved so why do I have to spend my energy in telling God how much he means to me?

Many reading this meditation have a common belief in the Heidelberg Catechism which states in Lord's Day number 1:

What is your only comfort in life and in death?

A. That I am not my own, but belong body and soul, in life and in death to my faithful Savior, Jesus Christ.

This same response closes with "because I belong to him, Christ by his Holy Spirit assures me of eternal life and makes me wholeheartedly willing and ready from now on to live for him.

Christianity is not a belief that one embraces and then rests upon one's laurels. It is however, a belief that we, on a daily basis, make every attempt to live for our Lord and Savior Jesus Christ in all of our speech and actions.

Being active in our gratitude for God's salvation, our lives will be seen by others as lives filled with goodness, knowledge, self-control, brotherly kindness and love. We are then making our calling and election sure. In so doing we shall prevail. "Well done thou good and faithful servant" will be our greeting when we enter into our eternal reward by our Lord and savior Jesus Christ.

Prayer:
Lord, I want to live a life of active gratitude for your wonderful salvation! Forgive my times of ungratefulness. Amen

Brush Strokes

² Count it all joy, my brothers,[a] when you meet trials of various kinds, ³ for you know that the testing of your faith produces steadfastness. ⁴ And let steadfastness have its full effect, that you may be perfect and complete, lacking in nothing.
⁵ If any of you lacks wisdom, let him ask God, who gives generously to all without reproach, and it will be given him. ⁶ But let him ask in faith, with no doubting, for the one who doubts is like a wave of the sea that is driven and tossed by the wind. ⁷ For that person must not suppose that he will receive anything from the Lord; ⁸ he is a double-minded man, unstable in all his ways.
⁹ Let the lowly brother boast in his exaltation, ¹⁰ and the rich in his humiliation, because like a flower of the grass[b] he will pass away. ¹¹ For the sun rises with its scorching heat and withers the grass; its flower falls, and its beauty perishes. So also will the rich man fade away in the midst of his pursuits.
James 1:2-11

Brush strokes are those events in our lives that happen to us. They are the events that we really have very little to do with their occurrence. They are the events which God allows to take place in our lives. We are "dealt a hand of cards". Our response is the theme of this brief meditation.

The brush strokes which happens to everyone is aging. Some of us are in the process of living beyond the ages of our ancestors. To many, this is a blessing in that we have a golden opportunity to live out our "bucket list" in two ways. One, for those things such as travel, visiting relatives and friends that during our working years there was just not enough time to efficiently visit and or travel. E-Mail, phone calls and Christmas Cards filled the gaps.

Another benefit of aging in good health is the time to "give back" to our families, churches and favorite missions our time and a greater percentage of our resources than we did prior to retirement.

Conversely, a brush stroke of a life shortening diagnosis inexorably places us on a shortened horizon (similar to our aging friends). Our horizon of time is now a brush stroke that is being painted with shorter and more rapids strokes.

Just take a moment and with personal introspection, attempt to ascertain what the master painter is depicting upon the easel of your individual life. Whether aging or in diminishing health, the sunset of your life is becoming more vivid. Just how do you want the painting of your life to appear? Yes, you can help to complete the brush strokes.

God bless you as you add color and light to the painting of your life. We know the absolutes of life such as death and eternity are coming. We can influence the variables!

Prayer:
Come soon, Lord Jesus come quickly! Amen

Jesus Calling

And the Lord came and stood, calling as at other times "Samuel! Samuel!" And Samuel said "speak, for your servant hears." Then the Lord said to Samuel "Behold, I am about to do a thing in Israel at which the two ears of everyone who hears it will tingle. On that day I will fulfill against Eli all that I have spoken concerning his house, from beginning to end. And I declare to him that I am about to punish his house forever, for iniquity that he knew, because his sons were blaspheming God, and he did not restrain them. Therefore, I swear to the house of Eli that the iniquity of Eli's house shall not be atoned for by sacrifice or offering forever."

1 Samuel 3: 10-14

When my mother called to me by my nickname "Chuck" there was a bit of "wiggle room" in allowable response time. However, when she used my given name "Charles" there was no latitude allowed for my response. Obedience to mom was ASAP – STAT.

When Jesus called his disciples, their response was immediate. None of them hedged their response by asking for more time to consider Jesus' call. They literally left their employment and followed Jesus. Peter and Andrew were casting their fishing nets into the lake when Jesus said "come follow me and I will make you fishers of men." (Matt. 4:18-20) James and John were getting their nets ready and they dropped everything to follow Jesus. (Matt. 4:21-22)

Recognizing who's talking is essential in today's society. Call recognition is standard on most phones. However when God is calling us, it sometimes takes a while before we realize that God is trying to get our attention. It took Mary Magdalene some time at Jesus' tomb for her to recognize that it was Jesus who was talking to her. Also, Samuel needed coaching by Eli to realize that God wanted a conversation with him.

In our lives there have been situations where God was trying to get our attention and it took a period of time for us to realize that God was trying to communicate with us. God wanted to get a message through to us. Once we become aware of God's calling out to us, how are we going to respond? Samuel's response is a great model for us to use, "speak Lord, for your servant is listening."

Prayer:
Father, I'm open to your calling. Use me where I am now, use me where you want me to be and I will do whatever you want me to do. Amen

Christ The Living Stone

As you come to him, a living stone rejected by men but in the sight of God chosen and precious, 5 you yourselves like living stones are being built up as a spiritual house, to be a holy priesthood to offer spiritual sacrifices acceptable to God through Jesus Christ. 6 For it stands in scripture. Behold, I am laying in Zion a stone, a cornerstone chosen and precious, whoever believes in him will not be put to shame.

1 Peter 2:4-6

Jesus Christ is referenced in scripture as the good shepherd, lamb of God and chief cornerstone. Many names are utilized so that we can more clearly understand our relationship to the author and finisher of our salvation. In today's scripture Jesus is pictured as the cornerstone.

A stone resembles permanence, strength and stability. Jesus is the ultimate stone, he is the cornerstone of our faith. All of our hope of salvation is secured by the cornerstone, Jesus Christ.

This living stone, Jesus, is the security of our faith. Conversely, this living stone is the stumbling block of those who reject the offer of salvation.

Those who have accepted Jesus as the cornerstone of their faith are now called a chosen people. Responsibility is included with being one of God's people. We are expected to be living stones. We are to have the solidity of a stone, the permanence of a stone and the immovability of a stone.

Being a Christian involves visibility as living stones. We are image bearers of Jesus Christ who is the chief cornerstone. Seclusion is out of the question for living stones.

Prayer:
Father, as a living stone may my presence and lifestyle reflect you. Amen

Covering All Our Bases

So Paul, standing in midst of the Areophagus said: "Men of Athens, I perceive that in every way you are very religious. 23 For as I passed along and observed the objects of your worship, I found an altar with this inscription:" To the unknown God." What therefore you worship as unknown, this I proclaim to you. 24 The God who made the world and everything in it, being Lord of heaven and earth, does not live in temples made by man, 25 nor is served by human hands, as though he needed anything, since he himself gives to all mankind life and breath and everything. 26 And he made from one man every nation of mankind to live on the face of he earth, having determined allotted periods and the boundaries of their dwelling place, 27 that they should seek God and perhaps feel their way toward him and find him. Yet he is actually not far from each of us, 28 for "in him we live and move and have our being".
Acts 17:22-28a

Paul showed his creative side when he addressed the Areophagus in Athens. This body of intellectual heavyweights exercised civil and religious authority over the residents of Athens. When Paul looked around his surroundings and saw the many wooden and stone Gods that were in full view, he noticed that one bore a title of the Unknown God.

Think about Paul's tactful approach when he addresses the Areophagus. Instead of demonizing the many false

193

Gods on display, he zeros in on the Unknown God and explains that his God fills the slot of the Unknown God.

The mind set in Athens concerning the selection of their false gods was very similar to how we select the insurances that we purchase. We cover our exposures to financial loss that we can't afford to cover when losses are experienced by the law of large numbers. So, we buy insurance to cover our homes, contents, auto, liability, life, long term care etc.

Paul's acceptance in Athens was not great but he was allowed to continue his ministry. There is a lesson in Paul's approach to the Areopagus, we need to use our discretion as to how we let others know the good news of salvation. Our approach is not to utilize the gospel as a way to cover all our possible vulnerabilities but to trust in the only way to Jesus by belief and our changed lifestyle. However, coming to Jesus can't be on a piecemeal basis. It is a total commitment of everything we are and hope to be. Yes, Jesus wants our all; our thoughts, our goals, our lifestyle, our finances all without hedging. So, our allegiance to Jesus is primary. He is the only way to eternal reward in heaven, Are you in? Skid marks will be erased.

Prayer:
Father, a refrain resonates with me. Jesus is calling, tenderly calling for you and for me. Come home, come home you who are weary come home. May my life reflect your open invitation to come home. Amen

Covetous

*You shall not covet your neighbor's house; you shall not
covet your neighbor's wife, or his male servant, or his
female servant, or his ox, or his donkey, or anything
that is your neighbor's.*
Exodus 20:17

*Not that I am speaking of being in need, for I have
learned that whatever situation I am to be content. I
know how to be brought low, and I know how to
abound. In any and every circumstance, I have learned
the secret of facing plenty and hunger, abundance and
need. I can do all things through him who strengthens
me.*
Philippians 4:11-13

As I was considering the purchase of a different
automobile, it passed through my mind why was I
considering a different automobile. Was it need,
convenience, better gas mileage or perhaps was I
attempting to look good in the eyes of my friends? After
all, many of them were driving cars of similar class and
price of the auto which I was considering. Was I keeping
up with the Jones's?

Contentment is possibly one of the rarest terms that
would describe the average American citizen. Within
most of us there is a mostly hidden desire to want more

than we presently have. The things that most of want more of are usually material belongings such a a larger bank account, a larger portfolio, a larger house, more stylish clothes, more and longer vacations like those of some of our friends. The Saturday evening show on PBS featuring Mrs. "Bookay" is a classic depiction of the phenomena of those who lack contentment.

Sociologists have a classification for those of us who lack contentment. That term is conspicuous consumption. What others can see what we have on display is so very important to our state of contentment. If we don't have adequate holdings to display, then we can acquire them on a temporary basis by short term apparent ownership. Another way to temporarily assuage our lack of contentment is to make sure that we are seen in the company of the "right people".

Our society is structured with associations where membership is determined by a large annual fee and or private invitation. Even churches are structured by class of apparel (Sunday Best), adequate automobile, significant address, notable educational status and acceptable grooming.

When God gave Moses the ten commandments, coveting was listed as the 10th. When we lack contentment, we really are quite guilty of coveting what we do not have. Conversely, the apostle Paul stated that whatever situation he was in he was content.

Life is similar to a balance scale. Contentment is on one side of the scale and covetous attitude is on the other side of the scale. I find myself on an unbalanced scale. Where are you on this scale of life?

Prayer:

Father, forgive my sins of wanting what I do not have. Instead, may my actions reflect contentment with the situation of life that you have allotted to me as your steward. Amen

Crucify Him

He said to the Jews "Behold your king!"15 They cried out "Away with him, away with him, crucify him!" Pilate said to them "Shall I crucify your King?" The chief priests answered, "We have no king but Caesar." 16 So he delivered him over to them to be crucified. John 19: 14b-16

The premise of this meditation is that "false news" is not a recent label but it was very apparent in the trial of Jesus when the Jews skewed the accusation that Jesus was guilty of blasphemy because he said that he was the "King of the Jews". The unspoken Jewish threat was that if you don't crucify Jesus then you don't support Caesar and we Jews support Caesar. Pilate then goes on to make a "politically correct" decision because if he didn't support Caesar the loss of his position was predictable as a minimum punishment for insubordination to Caesar.

Turning right on a red light with zero oncoming traffic from any direction seemed to be totally logical. However, the policeman that pulled me over asked if I had read the signs posted along one of Grand Rapid's busiest streets that right turns on red were forbidden. I gulped and turned a shade of red that I had turned on and expected an expensive ticket. However, grace prevailed, and the officer proceeded to advise me to go on my way with only his verbal warning. We then had a nice conversation concerning the model and make of my "ride".

The prophetic signs were posted all through the scriptures that Jesus was going to be lifted up and crucified and to die to bear the sins of mankind. How could we not see the signs? It's easy to direct an accusatory finger of blame toward the Jews. What would have been our stance if we had spent a lifetime as a devout Jew? Perhaps we would have been a worshiping Jew, very comfortable in our own legalistic skin of outward obedience to the law and the prophets. Certainly, this Jesus was just "false news" who came into Jerusalem on a donkey. Our Jesus would have come with an entourage of soldiers in parade dress, royal stallions as their mounts and our King Jesus would have followed in a shiny chariot.

Perhaps some of us are falling victim to the gospel message in a watered-down state. Let's face it, it's more comfortable to believe that there are many paths to salvation. That there is a God that "looks the other way" when we persist in some behavior that isn't public and is so very enjoyable. You get the idea. False gospel messages are all around us. It's time to look for the signs in the scriptures.

Prayer: *Father forgive me for my cavalier attitude toward you. When I see Jesus on the cross, I see the real news. You sacrificed your son for my sins, and I bow in repentance. I'm yours Lord. Amen*

Finances

So early in the morning Jacob took the stone that he had put under his head and set it up for a pillar and poured oil on the top of it.19 He called the name of that place Bethel, but the name of that city was Luz at the first.20 Then Jacob made a vow, saying "If God will be with me and will keep me in this way that I go, and will give me bread to eat and clothing to wear, 21 so that I come again to my father's house in peace, then the Lord shall be my God, 22 and this stone, which I have set up as a pillar, shall be God's house. And all that you give me I will give a tenth to you."
Genesis 28:18-22

Also, suggested scripture: Mal. 3:8-10

The last thing to be devoted to the Lord is one's wallet. You have probably heard fellow Christians make comments attesting to the same dynamics. There are many people who are Christians that give only a very small percentage of their earnings to the Lord. George Barna speaks to this state of affairs in many of his analytical publications stating that the rough average of giving from one's income is about 3%. One out of every ten church attending Christians donate at least 10% of their income. More than 30% claim to do so.

The reason for giving at such a low level is not known. It can only be answered accurately between the giver and God. The underlying answer has to do with one's relationship to God. It's probably quite accurate to say that an analysis of one's checkbook will reflect where an individual is with God.

Sermons are seldom preached using scripture as a sound basis to describe tithing in the biblical mandate of 10%. It is rather common for preachers to attempt to motivate their parishioners to increase their giving by 1 or 2%. Their thinking is that we will "turn off" the audience if we ask people to obey what the Bible plainly outlines.

Where one is at with God is reflected in what is deemed not only by the state of the checkbook, but it is precisely reflected in the giver's heart. How fellow Christians observe our giving is perhaps a major motivation to donate to causes that will reflect to others that we are faithful givers. Peer approval doesn't pass for cementing our relationship with our savior.

So now it is the end of the week and I'm making out a check to the church and there is also a small pile of worthwhile causes on my desk that are in competition for my resources. So how do I decide? As I prayerfully consider the parameters of my obligation, I'm suddenly hit with the realization that this checkbook isn't mine at all. I'm just returning to God what he has allocated to me as one of His stewards.

Prayer:
Forgive me Father for even thinking that it's mine. I'm just a steward of what you have given to me to allocate. Amen

Fishermen/Disciples

[18] While walking by the Sea of Galilee, he saw two brothers, Simon (who is called Peter) and Andrew his brother, casting a net into the sea, for they were fishermen. [19] And he said to them, "Follow me, and I will make you fishers of men."[a] [20] Immediately they left their nets and followed him. [21] And going on from there he saw two other brothers, James the son of Zebedee and John his brother, in the boat with Zebedee their father, mending their nets, and he called them. [22] Immediately they left the boat and their father and followed him.

Matthew 4:18-22

The first disciples that Jesus chose were Peter, Andrew, James, and John. Fishing was their family business. It was their sole source of financial income.

It is significant that when Jesus called them, that each one of them responded positively, immediately. There was no reticence no "I'll think about it and get back to you".

What an unusual set of events in that without applications, oral questioning of Jesus or resume's, Jesus selected 4 fishermen. Today, there would be a complete sequence of standard hiring procedures and after the traditional two interviews there would be the promise of a job. Bear in mind that the new job was without pay, no usual benefits, no promise of reward later on and family had to be left behind.

Yet Jesus had an ultimate advantage over today's usual hiring practices in that he knew their hearts and their ability to focus on life's goals in the presence of difficult odds.

So why were the fishermen the first to be selected over the more educated, teachers, tax collectors etc.? Perhaps fisherman share a commonality of hard work, patience, focus, open to new methods etc.

The first four disciples typically worked all night when the fish were schooling to predictable areas and depths. Fishing successfully requires a fisherman to "go where the fish are" The work entailed fishing all night, cleaning the fish, mending the nets and marketing the catch. Their new job of fishing for men was going to utilize similar hard work, focus, long hours and learning new methods of fishing for men with a new gospel. No more, obey the law only and you'll be rewarded.

Upon one occasion, Jesus was preaching from Peter's boat because the crowd was so large and pressing Jesus toward the sea behind him. Peter's boat didn't even smell like fish because the previous night of fishing yielded zero fish. So, after Jesus finished preaching, he recommended to Peter that he fish in deeper water. Had I been Peter, I might have not listened to the advice of a non-fisherman. Peter however said, "because it is you who is asking, we'll give it a try." The response was not one, but two overloaded boats of fish.

What a lesson for the seasoned fishers of fish and now rookie fishers of men.

So how about your life experiences. Has Jesus been directing your boat? If not, could it be that you have not invited him into the aspects of your life in the workplace? Try taking Jesus to work with you. You'll be amazed that your fishing for men might become an intentional aspect of where you go to earn a living.

Prayer:
Jesus, use me to make a difference for you in the workplace. I'll be more intentional in "fishing" for your kingdom. Amen

Following Jesus

"Follow me and I will make you fishers of men".
Immediately they left their nets and they followed him.
Matthew 4:19-20

Peek-a-boo is one of the first games we play with our very young children, much to our mutual delight. As children mature, hide-and seek is a game that children enjoy.

In each child's game there is an element of hiding and revealing. When one comes out of hiding there are cries of delight at being found and the hiding element is over.

Jesus called the brothers Peter and Andrew to be his disciples right as they were fishing. Jesus' invitation to "come follow me and I will make you fishers of men." The invitation was not met with hesitation but both brothers dropped their nets and immediately followed Jesus.

Being called by Jesus to be a disciple, by definition, was open acceptance to join Jesus band of followers. To follow as a disciple meant a 24/7 schedule of learning and doing, observing, listening and arriving at a point of irreversible belief and following the directions of the Great Commission uttered at Jesus' ascension.

"All authority in heaven and on earth has been given to me. [19] Go therefore and make disciples of all nations, baptizing them in[a] the name of the Father and of the Son and of the Holy Spirit, [20] teaching them to observe all that I have commanded you. And behold, I am with you always, to the end of the age."

Matthew 28:18b-20

There is no such thing recognized as acceptable Christian behavior to be a follower of Jesus in hiding. By definition, such a person shows Christian behavior in speech and behavior to other church members and not to those secular acquaintances. It is time to publicly follow Jesus ASAP. Jesus is saying to you and to me as he said to his disciples "come follow me". We don't know how much time will be allocated for us to be obedient to the Great Commission. So, let's repent and follow Jesus now.

Prayer:
Father forgive my sin of hiding the salt and light of your gospel from all of the people I come into contact with. May I be consistent in representing you by my actions and intentional speech. Amen

Foundation

Sanctify them in the truth; your word is truth.
John 17:17

Where are you coming from? This is a question in the minds of Bible believing Christians when they hear or observe what is contrary to what is definitely not found in the scriptures.

Those who have been through a basic course in philosophy have probably been faced with the premise that there is no such thing as absolute truth. All philosophies and opinions are open to change to meet the demands of current societal thinking. Our country has a constitution which is a living document or a document of truth as observed by the supreme court which determines whether the constitution is law subject to amendment or law subject to change because it is a moving document.

Christians however universally believe that the Bible is the inspired Word of God. That it is the source of absolute truth. Man's hope of eternal life is based upon this truth. There are those among us who wish to change the truth of the Bible to fit their own personal feelings which are usually prefaced by "My God wouldn't" and one can fill in the blanks following such a preface which is basically idolatry because God's Word is being replaced with personal opinions to fit into one's comfort zones.

The holiness of God is thus avoided when one changes what is clear in the scriptures. This God is the source of absolute truth. It is the foundation upon which Christians are united. It is the cornerstone of Christian belief.

Those who modify God's Word are basically saying that if God were only seeing society as I see it then he would change the language of the Bible to meet societies' current needs. Such thinking leads to some of the following heresies:

There are multiple paths of salvation. A singular path is outmoded.

Marriage is not just between a man and a woman, but it can also include one of the same sex.

One's gender is subject to one's wants. It is not determined by physical structure.

Human life is decided at birth. It is a mother's decision to abort or to give birth.

There are pastors who never preach on the absolutes of the Bible and their scriptural omission places their ministry in the heresy category.

Where are you coming from? Is the Bible your source of absolute truth? Is it the foundation for your present and future eternal life?

Prayer: *Eternal absolute God. I simply love you and will by my words and behavior point others to the absolute truth. Amen*

Games

So, whether you eat or drink or whatever you do, do all to the glory of God.
I Corinthians 10:31

"Peek a boo" is a delightful early game played with children who are in the process of discovering their world around them. It's a noisy atmosphere with many infant giggles.

A later learned game is "Hide and Seek". Generations readily carry on these children's games with non-waning interest.

Later on in life, deception takes on a more sophisticated and somewhat tainted appearance. It's easy to avoid extra effort at our workplaces by working with less effort or reporting our hours to be more than they really are. Altered income tax reporting is another adult game of deception. Also, embellishment in the marketing area is another adult game of "hide and seek".

In addition, some of us hide our behaviors to our friends and even families when those behaviors are less than what we are wanting others to view.

In conclusion, some Christians by name are living compartmentalized lives. Yet we know that in all of life we are to live to the glory of God.

Prayer: *Father forgive the sins of my behavior that I try to hide from you and others. May my future actions reflect that I'm without deception and totally transparent. Amen*

God's Presence

O come, let us sing to the Lord; let us make a joyful noise to the rock of our salvation! 2 Let us come into his presence with thanksgiving; let us make a joyful noise to him with songs of praise!

Psalm 95: 1-2

The presence of God is a topic which escapes most sermons and Bible studies. The rationale is most probably that the scope of the topic is too broad to be discussed except in a very general basis and is therefore avoided. The rationale for this attempt to look at the concept of God's Presence is because it was of such importance to God that he went into great detail as to the holiness, awareness, and the passing on of the entire concept to future generations. With this broad introduction, let's look at where it all started to be introduced to the understanding of mankind.

Moses became acutely aware of the presence of God when confronted with a burning bush. God spoke directly to Moses in a most unique fashion because Moses had passed all his interviews and was now being selected to head up the exodus of the chosen people.

God further demonstrated his presence in the form of a pillar of cloud during the daytime and a pillar of fire by night for direction and assurance of His presence on a 24/7 basis.

God further made sure that the Israelites never forgot His nearness in the elaborate details of the Ark of the Covenant. This was the ongoing symbol of God's presence with His people.

Today, in our posh lifestyle, the presence of God does not have the emphasis that it once had. It appears that we are so self-sufficient that we are not aware of the ongoing presence of God. Yes, we are reminded of God's closeness when we worship together. Also, when we are facing life's trials we are in need of the prayers and support of Christian friends so we are drawn into God's presence.

When we look at today's society, what do we see? Perhaps if we see the throngs of people around us as Jesus sees them then we see a great need for salvation of the masses. Just perhaps, we are the only presence of God that society will see. In our efforts to be "salt and light" let's be that presence of God in our relationships.

Prayer:
Father, we ask your forgiveness for our uncaring attitudes toward others that need you for their eternity. Amen

211

Gone Fishing

A Bible Study leader attempting to insert humor into Revelations 21:1 *(Then I saw a new heaven and a new earth; for the first heaven and the first earth had passed away, and the sea was no more)* announced that there would be no oceans or lakes is Heaven. He let that thought just lie there on the surface without reading further where in revelations 22:1-8 there is a beautiful depiction of a river, a garden, a pure outdoor lovers' euphoria.

As a Walter Mitty of the fishing set, my first thought was that if I can't fish in Heaven, what am I going to do with my recreational time? (Sinful thought) My thoughts then went back some decades when my son was putting his two eldest sons to bed in their bunk beds. The oldest son said: "Dad, can I give my heart to Jesus right now?" My son immediately responded that "of course" thinking that his evening sermon had found rich soil. So the "sinner's prayer" was uttered by my grandson in the midst of tears of great joy. However, out of the bottom bunk came the question" Dad, are there toys in Heaven?" My son responded that "yes probably, but he couldn't be absolutely sure. "The immediate lower bunk response indicated that his decision was pending his dad finding out for sure. Strange how history repeats itself in the similar thinking of an old grandpa.

As you contemplate your spiritual pulse, is your internal soul's GPS calibrated for that Garden of Life? My parting advice comes from the refrain that I noted from a choir in a Baptist college: "I'm yours Lord, everything I've got, everything I'm not, I'm yours."

I'll take my walleye lightly dusted and pan seared right after I complete the bass part of the Hallelujah Chorus.

Prayer:
Father, I look forward to that great eternity with you. I can't find words to express my anticipation. Amen

I Am Who I Am

*Then Moses said to God, "If I come to the people of
Israel and say to them, "The God of your fathers has
sent me to you, and they ask me, What is his name?
what shall I say to them?"14 God said to Moses, "I Am
Who I Am." And he said ,"Say this to the people of
Israel: "I Am has sent me to you"15 God also said to
Moses, "Say this to the people of Israel: "The Lord, the
God of your fathers, the God of Abraham, the God of
Isaac, and the God of Jacob, has sent me to you. This is
my name forever, and thus I am to be remembered
throughout all generations.
Exodus 3:13-15*

'I Am that I Am' refers to the divine name Yahweh, many
meanings are built into the name Yahweh.

- God is not to be dependent upon anything.
  Therefore, God is self-existent.
- God is the creator and governor of all that exists or
  has existed.
- God does not change.
- God is eternal.
- God will always be with us.

Moses certainly knew the name of God, but he needed to
hear the voice of God stating do you really know who I
am? Yes, "I Am That I Am".

How laughable when we encounter someone so puffed up with their feelings of self-importance that they say, "do you know who I am"? Really?

God wanted us to respect his name to the point that he made a special commandment so that we would treat his name with awe and reverence.

You shall not take the name of the Lord your God in vain, for the Lord will not hold him guiltless who takes his name in vain. Exodus 20:7

So many times, we as Christians do not accurately reflect the name of the God who we represent. The 3rd commandment draws focus on how we are to reflect God's name. When we take God's name in vain to emphasize our speech, we are throwing an inconsistency to those hearing our feeble attempts at emphasis.

How confusing our blue speech must be to those who are within earshot of adding God's name to our stories and jokes. Just think of how our witness has become confusing and negative to those we are inviting to worship with us.

The Great I Am has not changed and he is expecting us to accurately represent him.

Prayer: *Oh, Great I Am, forgive my sins of not treating your name with the utmost respect and reverent honor. As I interact with others also made in your image, may my life reflect you the Great I Am. Amen*

Idolatry

"You shall not make for yourself a carved image, or any likeness of anything that is in heaven above, or that is in the earth beneath, or that is in the water under the earth. 5 You shall not bow down to them or serve them, for I the Lord your God am a jealous God visiting the iniquity of the fathers on the children to the third and fourth generation of those who hate me, 6 but showing steadfast love to thousands of those who love me and keep my commandments.
Exodus 20:4-6.

The Old Testament refers to idols as something visual which was worshiped as a god. When idols are discussed, they are generally a symbol carved by man.

Within each of us is a "god hunger". We seek to give adoration to something that is all important to us. So, it was very logical that early cultures would worship something beyond themselves.

In today's society, idolatry is seldom discussed because our idols have a different appearance. We have "progressed" so that our idols are our own self sufficiency. We idolize our abilities to surround ourselves with creature comforts. The accumulation of things gives us a sense of security. When we are surrounded by our emergency fund, our 401K, our definable pension plan, our homes, cars, boats, cottages etc. our idols are apparent.

You see, we've got all the bases covered. We are "self-made people" Really?

No idols in today's culture? To the contrary, we are all sufficient because of our wealth and pseudo security. We bow down to anything that replaces God. We have an affinity to be in the inner circle of those individuals that are really wealthy.

However, when situations beyond our control such as financial downturns, illness, death of a loved one or any of the "valleys of life" our idols not only lose their luster but they really become meaningless.

Where are you at right now? Got any idols?

Little children, "keep yourselves from idols".
I John 5:21

Prayer: *Lord, forgive my idolatry. I'm yours forever. Amen*

Jars of Clay

The word that came to Jeremiah from the Lord; 2 "Arise, and go down to the potter's house, and there I will let you hear my words." 3 So I went down to the potter's house, and there I will let you hear my words." So I went down to the potter's house and there he was working at his wheel.4 And the vessel he was making of clay was spoiled in the potter's hand, and he reworked it into another vessel, as it seemed good to the potter to do.
Jeremiah 18:1-4
The precious the sons of Zion, once worth their weight in fine gold, how they are regarded   as earthen pots, the work of the potter's hands!
Lamentations 4:2

Clay is an old reliable building product. It's been used to make bricks for many, many years. Israel used clay in their years of enslavement in Egypt. American Indians used it to build their dwellings. Today it is found in building supplies and as a "go slow" roadbed on some local streets. Yes, it's even the base ingredient of Kitty Litter.

So, clay is noted for its strength. It's resistant to weather and erosion. It is also used to line collection lagoons, rural water treatment plants in that it retains the water to allow for evaporation and slow leaching into underground soil.

For today's meditation, let's consider clay as a flexible product that is formed into a container, a pot if you will. The shape, size and durability is at the design of the potter (God).

For our present consideration consider yourself as a container (a pot) which is being formed by the almighty potter. It makes for a great illustration but is it consistently true in your lives?

A pot has contents. These contents are our histories of life experiences both trivial and in depth, spiritual and secular.

Speaking for myself, I must confess that this old jar of clay is cracked and worn. It is my ongoing challenge to purposefully pour out the contents as I proceed on life's journey. The contents of your personal jar of clay will overflow. What flows out is sometimes intentional and sometimes at random. But rest assured that the contents are being seen, absorbed and evaluated by the great cloud of witnesses that surround us daily.
Some brief and obvious conclusions:
1. How intentional are you in sharing the contents of your personal jar?
2. Do you sometimes share the ingredients in an inappropriate manner such as a cutting remark or a joke that is a bit on the blue side?
3. What's your relationship with the potter?
4. When was the last time on the potter's wheel? This should be a regular and intentional time of "mold me and make me after your will".

5. Lamentations 4:2 sums it up well:
The precious sons of Zion,
worth their weight in fine gold,
how they are regarded as earthen pots,
the work of a potter's hands!

Prayer:
Have thine own way, Lord! Have thine own way! Thou art the Potter; I am the clay. Mold me and make me after thy will, while I am waiting yielded and still. Amen

Joseph's Forgiveness

Say to Joseph, "Please forgive the transgression of your brothers and their sin, because they did evil to you. "And now please forgive the transgression of the servants of the God of your father." Joseph wept when they spoke to him. 18 His bothers came and fell down before him and "Behold we are your servants." 19 But Joseph said to them "Do not fear, for am I in the place of God? 20 As for you, you meant evil against me, but God meant it for good, to bring it about that many people should be kept alive, as they are today. 21 So do not fear, I will provide for you and your little ones."
Genesis 50:17-21a

Have you had the experience of knowing someone who carried a grudge to the end of their life? Personally, I have witnessed those dynamics of a grudge and have observed that it just doesn't go away. It is apparently savored and ruminated over by the one holding the grudge and seems to build in intensity over the life span of the individual.

Others when they feel and/or observe that they have been wronged impose a "silent treatment" upon the one who has erred. Needless to say, this treatment greatly curtails communication and negates forgiveness for the duration of the painful silence.

By contrast, it is refreshing to observe people who forgive and don't bring it up again. Joseph, in today's story, was an example of great forgiveness. He certainly had cause to hold a grudge. His brothers had faked his death, lied to their father, and sold Joseph to a caravan of Ishmaelites who were on their way to Egypt.

After all is said and done, Joseph is in control of seven years of stored harvest. He is in charge of apportioning out the harvest on an as needed basis. The recipients are the Egyptians and his father's household. What a golden opportunity for a grudge or at least a silent treatment. Instead, he welcomes the reunion of a dysfunctional family complete with a free move to Egypt in a choice neighborhood.

Where are you at in your relationships? Are you a blessing by your forgiving attitude or are you relishing the sweet savor of a grudge that intensifies as you dwell upon it and enhance it.?

A part of the Lord's Prayer sums it up perfectly, "forgive us our debts as we forgive our debtors".

Prayer: *Father, soften us that we may go and forgive our brother so that our forgiveness reflects your love for us who need forgiveness. Amen*

Last Words

One of the criminals who were hanged railed at him, saying, "Are you not the Christ? Save yourself and us! 40 But the other rebuked him, saying "Do you not fear God, since you are under the same sentence of condemnation?41 And we indeed justly, for we are receiving the due rewards of our deeds; but this man has done nothing wrong." 42 And he said, "Jesus, remember me when you come into your kingdom." 43 And He said to him, "Truly, I say to you, today you will be with me in paradise."

Luke 23:39-43

On the severe bleak hillside called Golgotha (the place of a skull) Jesus was led to be crucified between two robbers.

While on the cross, being held vertical by spikes driven into his feet and hands, Jesus speaks to the crowd that was gathered to lament Jesus' death.

When we are notified that a loved one is dying, it is quite common for immediate family and special friends to gather at the bedside of the one facing death. Not only are they gathered to say appropriate "goodbyes" but also to listen for any "last words" from the lips of the one who is entering eternal bliss.

As we age and/or are facing a life shortening illness, our thinking becomes more focused on how we will spend our last days on earth. Will they be filled with pain? Will

I be able to be mobile or will I need assistance with personal care? Fortunately, there are many options in today's world that can handle our personal care. It is at this point in time that the church can be of service in visiting and administering to some social needs and spiritual needs such as scripture reading and prayer.

This is not the time to make an assumption that just because the person dying has been a lifelong church member that they know for sure that they are entering heaven when they breathe their last. It is a wonderful opportunity to ask the dying person if they know for sure that they are going to enter heaven with Jesus. This will be a time for the person's last words to be those of positive assurance.

Jesus answered the one robber as he was dying that he would be with him in Paradise. What an assurance for all of us. Jesus forgives when we confess. Jesus saves even at the last minute; Jesus saves in spite of what society has condemned. We join Jesus as we breathe our last in our eternal home.

An old hymn comes to mind:
Blessed Assurance
Blessed assurance, Jesus is mine!
Oh, what a foretaste of glory divine!
Heir of salvation, purchase of God,
Born of His Spirit, washed in His blood.
This is my story; this is my song!
Amen

Listen Up

⁴ 'You yourselves have seen what I did to the Egyptians, and how I bore you on eagles' wings and brought you to myself.

Exodus 19:4

Are you paying attention? As a male spouse, I must confess that I don't listen carefully and completely. Too many times I reach conclusions before my spouse has finished her statement. My daily prayer is for me to slow down and listen!

Apparently, God had the same dilemma when he reminds the Israelites on how they had been led, fed and protected during the Exodus.

I must admit that many times I have been critical of the Jews for their incessant grumbling and general lack of not paying attention to God's protective actions. So God has to remind them how they have been carried on eagles wings. Yes, realistically, I probably would have joined them in their ongoing negativity.

So the question to each one of us is are you listening (paying attention) to God as He speaks to us regarding his constant care for us? Take a figurative step back and ask yourself are we really listening to what is necessary to live a thankful life.

As in all relationships, they are composed of give and take. They are built on the first step of listening. God wants us to "listen up". He is talking to us constantly in how he bears us up on eagles wings every second of our existence.

Just think by looking at your personal history. Did you listen? Enough said.

Prayer:
Father, forgive my rushing ahead and not listening to you speaking. Amen

designed by 🖌 freepik

Love One Another

"A new commandment I give to you, that you love one another: just as I have loved you, you also are to love one another. 35 By this all people will know that you are my disciples, if you have love for one another."
John 13:34-35

Many times, in my many years on this earth, I have mentally assessed someone incorrectly based upon the externals such as dress, body size, speech etc. However, later on, after becoming better acquainted with the individual, I discovered a most surprising person who was a humble servant of Jesus and was living a life of service to the kingdom.

Certainly, putting people into "boxes" based upon trite externals is not accurate and is definitely not scriptural. However, reaching out to people who we only know marginally and finding out who they "really are' is actually the best way to see them as Jesus sees them.

Mother Teresa's notable quote on this topic sums up the matter very nicely "if you judge people, you have no time to love them." As I survey my contacts and friends, it becomes readily apparent that my reaching out in love needs to become more urgent and more intentional. As I think back, there have been many opportunities that I have missed to reach out in love to others. Now miles, life, handicaps and eternity separate us and I can only look back with remorse over all the opportunities that I missed. However, there are many others that I can reach out to and extend an act and/or word of love.

Our actions need not be spectacular. A written thank you note, a phone call and even a text is something that will be treasured by the recipient. A ride to the store, church service or to the airport is another way to show that we care.

The pattern becomes apparent does it not that our acts of love, set the stage for more in depth conversations regarding personal needs, spiritual walk, eternal hope etc? About now, there should be thoughts going through your mind of what you can do to reach out in love and be like Jesus wants us to be.

Prayer:
Father, please forgive the times that I neglected to love others when I had the chance to do so. As of today, I'm intending to see others as you see them and to love and care for them. Amen

Love

⁴ Love is patient and kind; love does not envy or boast; it is not
arrogant ⁵ or rude. It does not insist on its own way; it is not
irritable or resentful;[b] ⁶ it does not rejoice at wrongdoing,
but rejoices with the truth. ⁷ Love bears all things, believes all
things, hopes all things, endures all things.
1 Corinthians 13:4-7.

Today's political speech is very noticeable in that
it lacks love. Truth in its absolute form is missing.
Statements are not necessarily true, but the media passes
their rhetoric off as fact. False news is all around us. Like
many other things we have become so accustomed to
people representing opposing views or political parties
thrashing their opponents without any regard for absolute
truth.

Yet Paul, in today's scripture says that we should
rejoice in truth. If we were to converse in absolute truth
in all of our speech, then we would never have our past
speech eroded by the truth as the years go by. True facts
and honest speech are especially important within the
marriage bond. Without absolute and complete truth in
relationships there would be a lack of trust and an erosion
of mutual allegiance.

In human relationships, when we trust each other
because we know that truth is the basis of all our

conversations, then we can endure the trials of life that come our way in the course of long-term relationships.

Needless to say, Jesus compared our trust for each other with that of a child. We need to be honest to the maximum for our relationships to endure.

When we are caught in a lie or partial truth, we lose our credibility with the person we lied to. Yet our heavenly father forgives us when we are less than honest in our speech and/or actions. It's totally mind blowing that God forgives us totally and completely when we come to him and ask for forgiveness.

The "however" you've been waiting to read about is that we are forgiven in direct proportion to our level of forgiveness that we allocate to those who have sinned against us. The Lord's Prayer rings in my ears with the words "forgive us our debts as we also have forgiven our debtors." We can't hold a grudge and expect God to forgive us when we fail to forgive others.

So it comes down to love in our speech and actions. So, my friends, go in peace with pure speech and actions and answer positively to our Master's question to Peter, "Lovest thou me?"

Prayer:
Father in Heaven you know that I love you. My words and actions as of right now will attest to my promise. Amen

Lukewarm

15 "'I know your works: you are neither cold nor hot. Would that you were either cold or hot! 16 So, because you are lukewarm, and neither hot nor cold, I will spit you out of my mouth. 17 For you say, I am rich, I have prospered, and I need nothing, not realizing that you are wretched, pitiable, poor, blind, and naked. 18 I counsel you to buy from me gold refined by fire, so that you may be rich, and white garments so that you may clothe yourself and the shame of your nakedness may not be seen, and salve to anoint your eyes, so that you may see. 19 Those whom I love, I reprove and discipline, so be zealous and repent. 20 Behold, I stand at the door and knock. If anyone hears my voice and opens the door, I will come in to him and eat with him, and he with me. 21 The one who conquers, I will grant him to sit with me on my throne, as I also conquered and sat down with my Father on his throne. 22 He who has an ear, let him hear what the Spirit says to the churches.'"

Revelation 3:15-22

Being lukewarm is intolerable in whatever setting it is found. Lukewarm in a marriage aptly describes a dead relationship. In fact being lukewarm is a negative in any relationship.

So the church of Laodicea is being critiqued by the Amen. The Hebrew word for Truth. The fault of the church at Laodicea is that in their own eyes, they had it made. Who needs God when you have it all? They had wealth because of their flourishing textile industry, a corner on the market for the best eye salve around and large portfolios.

In our society we are under constant scrutiny. Lukewarm attitudes just "don't fly". Employees with ho hum attitudes are not successful in the workplace. Promotions typically are awarded to those who are at least moderately aggressive and caring of others.

Today in our society, there is the perfect atmosphere for us to be given the lukewarm diagnosis. We have "it made" in our physical needs being met. We have all the food, shelter etc. that is necessary and then some. So we have a situation very similar to the church at Laodicea. It is difficult to see our spiritual need when we are surrounded in creature comforts.

Jesus, the great Amen, is standing at the doors of our hearts and knocking. Notice, he does not forcefully enter. He's knocking – are you listening? His message is the same for each one of us. "I love you and I'm knocking and knocking. Don't let me just keep knocking" In fact Jesus might have to allow the entry of some of life's negatives to get our attention. The unasked question is what is it going to take? We are not really controlling our destinies. We are merely the stewards of what God has entrusted to us. What's it going to take?

Prayer:
Father, we love you. Forgive us for being so self-assured that we haven't been attentive to your knocking. Today, we pledge to answer your knocking at our doors. Amen

Mission Model

Many Samaritans from that town believed in him because of the woman' testimony, "He told me all that I ever did."40 So when the Samaritans came to him, they asked him to stay with them, and he stayed there two days. 41 And many more believed because of his word. 42 They said to the woman, "It is no longer because of what you said that we believe, for we have heard for ourselves, and know that this is indeed the Savior of the world."

John 4:39-42

The story of the Samaritan Woman is one of my favorite biblical stories. I see myself going along with the disciples in the traditional way of the Jews.

The Jews avoided contact with the Samaritans because to do so would make them ceremonially unclean. It was standard operating procedure to avoid "those Samaritans" whose Bible was only the Pentateuch. They worshiped on Mt. Gerazim which was holy to them because Moses had built an altar there. At one time, the Samaritans had built a temple there on the sacred mountain. According to the legalistic Jews, "those Samaritans" just didn't match up.

It would be unfair to criticize the disciples at this time because they were busy baptizing new believers in the more comfortable area of Judea. Jesus goes toward Samaria by himself to go where no self-respecting Jew would go.

Jesus doesn't start preaching in the town square but instead begins a relational type of ministry by asking a woman a who was drawing water from Jacob's deep (138') and cool well for a drink. Younger women visited the well in the heat of the day to avoid the many people who would draw water toward the end of the day. Now you are getting the picture, Jesus has a plan to begin a mission model for his disciples that features a relational setting. Yes, in fact the mission starts with a woman who was one of "those Samaritans".

Of course, Jesus knew what was going to take place by engaging the woman in a conversation and then steering the discussion into a very personal area involving the woman's marital past.

It is at this juncture of conversation that I have so often been guilty of avoiding a more in depth and meaningful conversation. My typical response in many cases has been a thank you and departed to go about my business right after the "drink of water".

You know "the rest of the story" a phrase made popular by the late Paul Harvey. Jesus gets involved with the woman's background and he introduces her to the "Living Water" as a natural outflow of the conversation. Then she tells the village about the Living Water.

The "elephant in the room" is where do you place yourself in how you are meeting the opportunities of outreach that you encounter? Jesus sees each individual as a soul that needs to hear the gospel. If you and I don't tell them, then who will?

Prayer

Father give us "eyes" to see our neighbors and friends as you see them. Forgive our sins of avoidance of the past. May we speak out as the Spirit nudges us. Amen

Numbering Our Days

[10] The years of our life are seventy,
or even by reason of strength eighty;
yet their span[a] is but toil and trouble;
they are soon gone, and we fly away.
[11] Who considers the power of your anger,
and your wrath according to the fear of you?
[12] So teach us to number our days
that we may get a heart of wisdom.

Psalm 90: 10-12

Numbering our days is a spiritual introspection of how we are utilizing our time spent on earth. We all deal with the absolute certainty that we will leave this earth either by death or resurrection when Jesus returns for his second coming.

When one looks at what God has given us it really comes down to two main categories of time and finances. Our finances can be measured by market value. However, the measuring of time is a bit more elusive in that we can't see into the future. So, we can only number our days in present market value in finances and our time is what we can do now.

As we age and/or as we are confronted with a life shortening illness, our horizon comes into a more immediate focus. We place greater emphasis on our remaining days on earth. So the numbering of our days becomes more urgent.

Many of us have numbered our days to the magic of those golden retirement years. Modern medicine, healthy diets and exercise has given more days to our expected life span. Now retirees are faced with more time to spend beyond their retirement from their main vocation. What a great opportunity to actually realize some of those things that have accumulated in our "bucket list". What a wonderful time to get involved in those ministries that feature feeding and clothing those who are in need. Also, mission opportunities are all around us.

Hourly workers usually have to report their hours worked to the management. Salaried workers are usually evaluated on their productivity. The question that remains is how will God analyze us when we arrive before his throne? Yes, our sins are forgiven if we have followed Jesus. What questions will be asked? The logical question will be how did we number our days. Needless to say our seashell collections, trip photos etc. won't be evaluated but how we numbered our days for the kingdom of God will be the main topic.

So where are you on that great continuum of numbering your days?

Prayer:

Father, from this day forward, I'll spend more attention to what you have made available to me for the furtherance of your kingdom. My times are in your hands. My monies will be allocated to your causes in a more deliberate fashion. Humbly, your servant. Amen

Obituary

*²³ Let us hold fast the confession of our hope without wavering,
for he who promised is faithful. ²⁴ And let us consider how to stir
up one another to love and good works, ²⁵ not neglecting to meet
together, as is the habit of some, but encouraging one another,
and all the more as you see the Day drawing near.*

Hebrews 10:23-25

We all are in the process of crafting our obituaries in that each day is bringing us one day closer to our eternal reward. Our experiences, speech and actions are being viewed by others even by those who will author our obituaries after we have passed on.

Most of us will not "take pen in hand" and actually write our own obituaries. It will then be incumbent upon our next of kin or our estate executor(s) to formulate the obituary. Typically, obituaries are complete with genealogy, educational background, career path, significant achievements, notable offices held etc.

So how do you want to be remembered? Be careful in the directions you might give to the authors of your obituary. One such person said to his heirs to just keep the obituary simple. Ir read

Name

Date of birth ------   Date of death

Buick for sale-- low mileage

All humor put aside, when we appear before our maker, our past achievements, financial status, community awards etc. will not be the criteria upon which we will be judged. The important facts will be upon a central theme which answers the ultimate question of "Did you love Jesus"?

[12] "And now, Israel, what does the LORD your God require of you, but to fear the LORD your God, to walk in all his ways, to love him, to serve the LORD your God with all your heart and with all your soul, [13] and to keep the commandments and statutes of the LORD, which I am commanding you today for your good?

Deuteronomy 10:12-13

So then if that is how we are to live then we will die in the Lord.

In closing, live today and everyday as if it is your last. May your obituary reflect what really mattered to you and to God.

Prayer:
Father nudge me through your Spirit when I become too self-centered and need to adjust my life's trajectory toward you instead of upon myself. Amen

Oh My God

OMG

[14] God said to Moses, "I AM WHO I AM."[a] And he said, "Say this to the people of Israel: 'I AM has sent me to you.'" [15] God also said to Moses, "Say this to the people of Israel: 'The LORD,[b] the God of your fathers, the God of Abraham, the God of Isaac, and the God of Jacob, has sent me to you.' This is my name forever, and thus I am to be remembered throughout all generations.

Exodus 3:14-15

"Oh My God" is probably one of the most heard expletives in everyday conversation and on television sitcoms. One can easily draw the conclusion that the use of God's name has been trivialized and is not looked upon with awe.

The use of the proper name for God began with God's instruction to Moses to tell Pharaoh that the name to use was "I Am". The use of the name as "I Am" meant that human comprehension could not adequately describe God. Jewish believers referred to God as YHWH. This name which could not be pronounced signified utmost reverence for God.

What a contrast to today's usage of God's name. Today it is common to hear God's name used as a curse word as an expletive to add emphasis.

Malcolm Boyd an Episcopal priest authored a prayer titled "Are You Running With Me Jesus" in 1965. His attempt to bring prayer into a meaningful relationship was aimed at a culture that was moving away from with God.

When I first heard the title of Pastor Boyd's prayers I was dismayed. My initial thought was that once again man's most holy efforts to talk with his Savior had been trivialized. Just the opposite was true. The prayer was a sincere attempt to get the culture to speak to God in earnest prayer.

So as far as the two issues of using God's name as a curse or as an attempt to add deep intent to one's speech there is not an acceptable balance with God. The 4th commandment given directly to Moses by God plainly states that the name of the Lord your God shall not be misused and anyone who does so will not be held guiltless.

So in all important relationships conversations are expressive of our inner thoughts and emotions. This is what our God expects of us, he wants to talk to us. Is your conversation with God a dated rhetoric that lacks speaking from the heart? How about letting God into your inner sanctum?

Prayer:
Father, in all the busyness of life whether running or walking, I want to deepen my relationship with you. Amen

Passing It On

¹⁷ O God, from my youth you have taught me,
and I still proclaim your wondrous deeds.
¹⁸ So even to old age and gray hairs,
O God, do not forsake me,
until I proclaim your might to another generation,
your power to all those to come.
Psalm 71:17-18

Many of us are in the golden years of life. Our mortal horizons are more apparent and shrinking moment by moment. Just sit back and close your eyes and recall where you are at in this moment of your life. How did you get to this point of your mortality? What events were milestones that shaped you and altered your spiritual journey?

Our schedules have been changed, We are no longer faced with the world of employment and its accompanying stresses, deadlines, quotas, payrolls, commuting etc. Our children and their children are now immersed in the busyness that once was ours.

Our present state of retirement might involve following the sun to avoid the cold and shoveling. Our family contacts might be fewer than we had hoped for because the hectic schedules of work, following sports, dramas, concerts etc. are taking up so much time that we just don't see our families as often as we would like. Also, many of us spend winters walking the warm beaches of the south and the feel of sand and warm seawater on our feet as we gather shells is mildly intoxicating.

Back to our recall of past experiences. Does your family know of those events that shaped your walk with Jesus? The milestones of your life that drew you closer to Jesus are they known for the impact they had upon you? We've all had those "come to Jesus" moments that brought us up short and moved our path more upward.

So it's time to pass it on. The stoic approach of past generations needs to be set aside. Its time to let our families know where we have been and how it has affected our walk with Jesus. Our families know our jokes and stories but do they know the real story of what has shaped and molded us in our walk toward our eternal destiny?

Prayer:

Father forgive my sin of not communicating your truths that have been a part of my life to my family. From now on, I will look for opportunities to share with those you have entrusted to my care and influence. Amen

Peter, An Enigma

*He said to them, "But who do you say that I am?" 16
Simon Peter replied " You are the Christ, the Son of the
living God." 17 And Jesus answered him, "Blessed are
you, Simon Bar-Jonah! For flesh and blood has not
revealed this to you, but my Father who is in heaven. 18
And I tell you, you are Peter, and on this rock I will
build my church, and the gates of hell shall not prevail
against it."*
Matthew 16:15-18

Assuming that we will know people in heaven that we know from our earthly relationships, one person that I will look up is Peter. Why? The answer is quite simple in that I see many of my responses to Jesus are very similar to that of Peter.

When Jesus asked his disciples, "who do people say that I am"? The response of the disciples ranged from Elijah, John the Baptist to Jeremiah. Jesus narrowed his question to "but who do you say that I am"?

Peter immediately responded "you are the Christ, the Son of the living God" Jesus acknowledged Peter's statement of faith by saying that Peter would be one upon whom the church would be built and that the gentiles would hear about Jesus from Peter, the Rock.

Yes, this is the same Peter who walked on water, who sliced off the high priest's ear, who denied Jesus when he was scared at Jesus trial. Do you see yourself yet in this enigma called Peter? I certainly have an affinity for Peter's actions and confession.

Fast forward to Acts 2 :14-40 and read Peter's impassioned sermon. This same Peter who acted in wild and impulsive ways was now utilizing that passionate personality to preach a sermon that brought the "house down on their knees" to accept the plan of salvation. Can you believe it? 3,000 souls crossed the line to embrace Jesus as the result of the Spirit within them and the inspired words of Peter.

Perhaps your initial response to Peter's great sermon might be a desire that we should have more preachers like Peter who would preach the unvarnished truth of the gospel without running their thoughts through a politically correct screen. Yes, there is a need for more pastors who would preach biblical truths without fear of criticism from liberal ears.

My take is that if Peter were having a cup of coffee with us and if he were asked what can be done about a society that avoids the topics of the bible that are absolute truths. His response might be similar to what God told Moses when he was trying to do an end run around the job of leading the exodus; "who made your mouth?"

Prayer:

Lord, we know better. Give us the courage to "step up to the plate" and share the truths that are within us. Your great command to go and make disciples rests upon our shoulders. We will <u>go</u> and <u>show</u> and <u>tell</u>. Amen

Prayer Life

And when they had entered, they went up to the
upper room, where they were staying, Peter and John
and James and Andrew, Philip and Thomas,
Bartholomew and Matthew, James the son of Alpheus
and Simon the Zealot and Judas the son of James. 14
All these with one accord were devoting themselves to
prayer, together with the women and Mary the mother
of Jesus, and his brothers.
Acts1:13-14

The disciples and other close group members were meeting for an extended period of time in the upper room in anticipation of the Spirit. One can almost feel the vibrancy of those prayers!

True confession time. My prayer life is weakest when my world is rosy and positive. When things are going my way, prayer is often not really thought out. It is an afterthought tacked on at the end of a busy day just before drifting off to sleep. It takes effort to focus my thoughts and to discipline my thinking to pray in greater depth.

Jesus is a model for where my prayer life should be headed. Jesus prayed to his Father. He needed to talk to him. I'll never completely understand why Jesus had to talk to his Father. My take is that Jesus' human nature needed refreshment through communication with God the Father.

So how should we pray?

Be intentional. Develop an ongoing list of prayer concerns. When asking God to forgive your sins, he expects you to be specific. My assumption is that many of our sins are those of avoiding opportunities to reach out to those in need of spiritual and/or physical needs.
Be sincere. Never tell someone that they are in our prayers when they are not.
Follow Jesus' example to pray often. To pray in an atmosphere that is void of distractions and to pray even when we are busy and tired.
Pray for those people on our radar that need our prayers. Pray for the government at all levels.

So, how's your prayer life? If it needs repair and improvement, then get into action without delay.

Prayer:
Father, my prayers are going to become more specific, sincere and intentional. Amen

Quakes and Winds

²³ Some went down to the sea in ships,
doing business on the great waters;
²⁴ they saw the deeds of the LORD,
his wondrous works in the deep.
²⁵ For he commanded and raised the stormy wind,
which lifted up the waves of the sea.
²⁶ They mounted up to heaven; they went down to the
depths;
their courage melted away in their evil plight;
²⁷ they reeled and staggered like drunken men
and were at their wits' end.[a]
²⁸ Then they cried to the LORD *in their trouble,*
and he delivered them from their distress.
²⁹ He made the storm be still,
and the waves of the sea were hushed.
³⁰ Then they were glad that the waters[b] *were quiet,*
and he brought them to their desired haven.

Psalm 107:23-30

When I was just a youngster, I heard a sermon that still speaks to me. Its title was "What do you do when the earthquake comes?"

I was absolutely rivetted by the topic because growing up in southern California, I had experienced a number of quakes ranging from minor hard to feel tremors to the larger ones that prevented walking over the rolling ground and was damaging to houses.

The quake that I remember most was when I was about 3-4 years old, my mother came running into my bedroom and literally threw her whole body over me. She could hear larger quakes a few seconds before they arrived. Her great sense of hearing saved me from debris that could have fallen. I looked over her shoulder and watched the walls sway back and forth.

The sermon stressed that our relationship with Jesus would protect us from the storms and quakes of life. Since hearing that sermon, I have been quite aware of my surroundings and have exercised caution to weather conditions before embarking on either water or land. Until recently.

My son and my grandson decided that we should fish a large body of water known for its oversupply of walleye. We felt that with a guide and a larger boat, what could go wrong? Then the morning of our first day, we received a phone call from our guide that winds were not in our favor and that gale winds were predicted later on in the day. We took a vote. In retrospect, I should have exercised veto power, but grandpa turned to "mush" and we decided that even if the deck was going to roll, we could catch a few and "run for home" just before the gale hit. Bad decision, the gale reared its ugly head when we were about 3 miles out without visible warning. 50 mph winds can cause a 22' boat to seem very small. Yet God was protecting three non-discerning fishermen. We obviously completed our day early and safely due to our God guiding that small craft.

The next day, the waters were calmer and the fishing was excellent. We stopped fishing at 11AM because we each had our limit of 8 walleye each.

It's interesting that the next day, at a celebratory reception for a college graduation, I overheard snippets of conversation referring only to grandpa's great fishing trip but no one mentioned the wind and our near fatal boat ride.

I've been musing about the quakes and winds of life. Some we can avoid if we pay attention to the signs and forecasts. However, in many of life's storms, we are blindsided, and we can't see the winds of life overtaking us. The marital betrayals, financial downturns, severe illnesses and fatal accidents are the valleys, storms and quakes of life.

It is mainly through the storms that God gets our undivided attention. Does he have your attention or are you just going through life and hoping for the best and being oblivious to the voice of God?

Prayer:
Father, I'm reminded of a closing sentence to an old hymn:
"May I hear thee say to me, fear not I will pilot thee."
Amen

Recognition of True Believers

But in the following instructions I do not commend you, because when you come together it is not for the better but for the worse. 18 For, in the first place when you come together as a church, I hear that there are divisions among you. And I believe it in part, 19 for there must be factions among you in order that those who are genuine among you may be recognized.
I Corinthians 11:17-19

When I go into the woods, I typically go in disguise. It is best to blend into one's environment and wear camouflage so that whatever prey I'm after has difficulty in recognizing that I'm not really an original part of the surroundings.

Our churches are normally more comfortable when our presence blends in with others in attendance. We can accurately categorize churches by their level of social class. This is illustrated by clothing styles, brand of cars owned, level of education and perceived accumulation of wealth.

In today's society, we are expected to tolerant of all beliefs, racial background, and social class. However, we are separated on Sunday in the pew. The Apostle Paul is speaking to the Corinthians recognizing that there are factions among them. Paul does not discourage factions, in fact he endorses them. Our differences are the most visible way to illustrate that we are true believers.

Could it be that to be recognized for our social status with all the trappings is not important. In fact, when our exterior veneer obscures where we stand scripturally, we are really Christians in camouflage.

So what is really important for us to be recognized as true believers? Let's start with where you stand on abortion, on same sex marriage and homosexuality. The list is not all inclusive but you catch the difference between Christians in disguise and outstanding Christians. So are these topics discussed, preached about or part of the Christian education in your church?

Prayer:

Father forgive my acceptance of the "comfortable pew". Give me the courage to stand up for you and what is biblically correct instead of what is socially correct. Amen

Samson for President

[32] And what more shall I say? For time would fail me to tell of Gideon, Barak, Samson, Jephthah, of David and Samuel and the prophets— [33] who through faith conquered kingdoms, enforced justice, obtained promises, stopped the mouths of lions, [34] quenched the power of fire, escaped the edge of the sword, were made strong out of weakness, became mighty in war, put foreign armies to flight. [35] Women received back their dead by resurrection. Some were tortured, refusing to accept release, so that they might rise again to a better life.

Hebrews 11:32-35

Samson was born into a time when the people of Israel did what was evil in the sight of the Lord. So God gave them into the governing hand of their arch rivals, the Philistines, for forty years.

An angel appears to Manoah of the tribe of Dan and predicts Samson's birth. He is to be a special person for God's singular assignment. He is to be a Nazarite from birth meaning that he is to be a teetotaler, no razor is to ever touch his person for a haircut or for a shave. His diet is to be only "ceremonial clean foods".

Needless to say, Samson was a change agent selected by God. He had the attention of the Israelites. Samson was the last judge of the Israelites before kings took over leadership.

Without going into great detail, the leadership of the judges did little to slow down the downward cycle of straying from God. Yet four of the judges are listed in Hebrews 11 among the heroes of faith.

So why the judges? It is apparent that God uses all classes of leadership to bring his chosen people to the point of sending Jesus to bear all their sins. So that through all types of leaders, Jesus enters history, Not one Jew could ever look backward to their history and say that if only a different type of leadership had been available they could have done it better.

No, God has a role in the selection of leaders. We in our republic have a unique system of governance that is totally unique. We have a vote, free speech and opinions. The global society is looking at America to show leadership. Now through prayer and Christian leadership, we can show excellence. Each person reading this meditation has a role. May God bless America!

Prayer:
Father you have given us great latitude in our own personal governance. We come to you for guidance in our attempts at leading. Amen

Saved by Grace

For by grace you have been saved through faith. And this is not your own doing; it is the gift of God, 9 not a result of works, so that no one may boast.
Ephesians 2:8-9

When one is facing a shortened life span due to aging, illness or the result of an accident, it is not unusual for such a person to question the surety of their salvation. A common reason voiced is that "I'm not good enough, I've done so many bad things and I don't seen how heaven is possible".

If you are experiencing similar doubts, please consider some biblical characters who have had some very serious sinful pasts and later experienced a promise of heaven and a completely changed lifestyle:

Rahab was a prostitute but was of the lineage of Christ.

Paul persecuted some of the early Christians and experienced a conversion and

became one of the most productive apostles.

Moses was guilty of murder and yet he led the Israelites to the promised land.

The thief on the cross next to Jesus, was promised heaven by his statement of belief.

Jesus can and will save any who call on his name and believe. His grace overpowers any of your doubts. Jesus will forgive all your sins regardless of your doubts. That is what it means to be saved by grace.

An old hymn fits our thoughts for today.

And I shall see Him face to face, and tell the story saved by grace;
and I shall see Him face to face and tell the story saved by grace.

Prayer: Father, if it was not for your grace not one of us could enter your heaven. Thank you, thank you for your loving grace. Amen

Self-Made Man

And I will say to my soul, "Soul you have ample goods laid up for many years; relax, eat, drink and be merry." 20 But God said to him "Fool! This night your soul is required of you and the things you have prepared whose will they be? 21 So is one who lays up treasure for himself and is not rich toward God."
Luke 12:19-21

A "self-made man" is one of the most sought after and valued descriptions of one who has risen to the upper echelons of financial achievement. People who have attained great wealth are surrounded by others who not only applaud the success of the wealthy but also find their own self-worth more clearly defined by being able to associate with the rich.

Sociologists have a descriptive identification called "conspicuous consumption" for those who try to keep up with those who are truly rich by being seen in the company of the wealthy, driving cars that stretch their finances, residing in houses beyond their means, wearing the latest in fashions etc. A banker friend of mine calls them "two-bit millionaires".

Rather than dwelling on the wealthy wannabes, the other side of those who have earned great wealth is that I live in a community that if it were not for the largesse of those whom God has blessed with great wealth there would not be the level of excellence in medicine, education, the arts and the alleviation of poverty.

There is an appreciation for those who have great wealth so that they are asked to serve on boards of hospitals, universities, colleges and other nonprofits etc. In addition, the media gives a lot of space in the press and spoken word to applaud the large gifts and other funding.

How difficult it must be to have achieved great wealth and to live in a humble relationship with one's God. Those who can so live, deserve the applause of the rest of society.

Certainly as has been outlined, great wealth can be and should be a blessing, not an obstacle to one's relationship with their Maker. Scripture has many passages which warn against the love of money taking over a person's allegiance to God.

It would appear that "having enough" is one of the most difficult equations to assess. Involved in one's personal assessment of how much should be retained versus how much should be shared is more of a spiritual decision than a mathematical equation. It is easier to assess a person's needs in the accumulation stage of the portfolio development and maintenance. Family recipients of one's estate need to be quantified. One's personal needs for the later years with assisted living and nursing home care all fall under the umbrella of accumulation assessment levels. Asset assessment might be labeled biblically as "filling one's barns"

Now once having established how much money is needed to meet family and personal needs, the more enjoyable aspect of filtering out where God wants us to allocate funds begins. Look around, the needs are beyond exhaustion.

As you evaluate the needs for funding, the use of what is "stored in your barns" becomes a vital part of your relationship with God. May this be a time that draws you closer to God. In this difficult time of stewardship may you grow nearer to Him not further away

Prayer: *Father we give back what is yours to others who are also yours. Amen*

Separation

Psalm 116:15
Precious in the sight of the Lord is the death of his
saints.

Isaiah 25:8
He will swallow up death forever;
and the Lord GOD will wipe away tears from all faces,

Romans 8 38-39
For I am sure that neither death nor life, nor angels nor
rulers, nor things present nor things   to come, nor
powers, nor height nor depth, nor anything else in all
creation, will be able to   separate us from the love of
God in Jesus Christ our Lord.

Today I'm feeling alone. Separated from a very
dear old friend. Death has parted us from our mutual
journey upon this earth. We are temporarily separated
from this "veil of tears".

The joys have been abundant. They ranged from
becoming acquainted when our children were very
young. We shared mutual church attendance, meetings
and wonderful times of after church coffee and bouncing
babies upon our laps.

Other joys have come in a small 12' fishing boat.
With primitive altered lures doctored up with our wives
bright red nail polish, we encountered our first three
salmon. These magnificent creatures weighed in on the
scales of the local grocery store at 90 lbs. Needless to say,
a lifelong addiction had just been created. This addiction

was validated every fishable Saturday morning. It put fish on the table and delight from the screaming reel from a king salmon trying to elude capture.

Fishing is a time of bonding and sharing memories that are indelible and cemented. In fact, time develops a sweet savor to the times of laughter, frustration over a missed netting effort, enjoying thermos coffee accompanied by a homemade sweet baked goodie.

Vocations, life's busyness separated us temporarily over the years. The occasional cell phone call reunited us as if no time had elapsed.

This temporary angst of separation will be replaced by a reuniting in glory. It remains a mystery as to what will be the venue of the future meeting. It might be the bass section of that great choir, or it might be collaboration over an educational curriculum, or just maybe meeting in a fishing boat trolling for the leviathans of the deep. I'll see you in eternity brother.

Prayer:
Father, thank you for placing Jack in my life. He made a difference quite beyond what words can express. Amen

Sexual Behavior

For this reason God gave them up to dishonorable passions. For their women exchanged natural relations for those that are contrary to nature; 27 and the men likewise gave up natural relations with women and were consumed with passion for one another, men committing shameless acts with men and receiving in themselves the due penalty for their error. 28 And since they did not see fit to acknowledge God, God gave them up to a debased mind to do what ought not to be done.

Romans 1:26-28

Paul begins to explain to his Roman audience that man's wickedness suppresses truth. In fact, since creation God's power and divine nature are so obvious that all of mankind is without excuse.

So, man has gone on into self-service in lieu of worshiping God. Consequently, man has entered into all kinds of sexual perversion.

Natural sexual behavior has been replaced by homosexuality and lesbianism. God has given them over to a depraved mind.

However, in today's society, it is essential to behave in a politically correct manner. Romans 1 and/or any other scripture passage condemning homosexuality is seldom utilized as the main topic of a sermon. In fact to denounce homosexuality as being sinful will bring down the wrath of the media, many society leaders and the LGBTQ. To criticize homosexual practice is to be labeled a homophobe.

Seriously, are we not allowed to denounce sin? Has God changed his mind to fit the mores of our decadent society?

The Apostle Paul did not pull any verbal punches when addressing his Roman audience. Where have all the courageous Christians gone? In fact, the slippery slope of Christian behavior has slid down to the point where mainline protestant denominations are in the process of defining marriage to not be between a man and a woman but rather marriage is between two consenting adults.

So how do we as Christians approach this societal problem of homosexuality? We need to embrace our homosexual friends just as we would any other sinner. We can do this by remaining their friend but not approving their behavior. We should invite them to join us in our church if we attend one that is biblical and not politically correct. Also, we do not join with them in their parades and celebrations that are aimed at "educating" the heterosexual straight society.

Our homosexual friends are our audience to hear the words of salvation. If we don't tell them, who will?

Prayer: *Father, forgive me for avoiding my homosexual friends and walking on the other side of the road. Amen*

Songs in the Night

You hold my eyelids open;
I am so troubled that I cannot speak.
I consider the days of old,
the years long ago.
I said "Let me remember my song in the night;
let me meditate in my heart."
Then my spirit made a diligent search:
Will the Lord spurn forever,
Has his steadfast love forever ceased?
Are his promises at an end for all time?
Has God forgotten to be gracious?
Has he in anger shut up his compassion?
Then I said, "I will appeal to this,
to the years of the right hand of the Most High."
Psalm 77:4-10

Many of us from time to time are faced with insomnia. The pharmaceutical industry has many answers for our nights of fitful sleep.

The causes for lack of sleep are many. Most of which are associated with the stresses of today's high-speed society. We are inundated with meetings, deadlines, jobs with hard to attain goals, crowded freeways etc. In addition, we text each other to communicate even to the point that it has affected our rate of word delivery when we are speaking. I believe

Solomon would have some words of wisdom for our harried lives. In Ecclesiastes 12:13 he states, ***"Fear God and keep his commandments, for this is the whole duty of man."***

In other words, intentionally reduce your stress filled lives by being more selective in how and when we spend our time. Get some physical exercise on a daily basis. Spend time in God's word on a regular basis and talk to your creator and savior in prayer.

A song in the night might be:

When peace like a river attendeth my way, when
sorrows like sea billows roll,
Whatever my lot, Thou hast taught me to say,
It is well, it is well with my soul".

Amen

Sunflowers

You are the light of the world. A city set on a hill cannot be hidden. 15 Nor do people light a lamp and put it under a basket, but on a stand, and it gives light to all in the house. 16 In the same way, let your light shine before others, so that they may see your good works and give glory to your Father who is in heaven.

Matthew 5: 14-16

Sunflowers always turn their blooms to face the sun. I was reminded of this fact of nature when while worshiping one Sunday morning, our entire congregation turned to face the only working projection screen situated in the rear part of the sanctuary. It got me to wondering what do people generally do when the light of their lives becomes obscure or completely darkened? Lights that can be darkened have to do with a dreaded diagnosis, failed employment, floundering relationships etc.

Many seek comfort in the onset of life's fading lights by overeating, alcohol use, drug use etc. Needless to say, none of these numbing agents are the solutions to the lowering of the lights in our lives. The gathering gloom of lowered light only continues and even intensifies.

Direct confrontation of the low light in our life is absolutely necessary to arrive at a solution.

The pattern of the necessity of light begins in creation by the words of God, "Let there be light". Light was given to the Israelites during their exodus from Egypt in the form of a pillar of fire. God's word is referred to as a lamp to one's feet and a light to one's path in Ps. 119:105. In Ephesians 5:8 we are instructed to walk as children of light.

As sunflowers turn to the sun as the source of light for growth and photosynthesis so we are to turn to God's word and the plan of salvation for our growth and spiritual nourishment.

Jesus, in the Sermon on the Mount brings light as a topic to illustrate how we are to reflect the light within us to the world. A city on a hill cannot be hidden. Nor do people light a lamp and hide it. Instead they place it upon a table so that the entire house is visible. So fellow Christians, where is your light of salvation pointing? Do others know where you are headed? Are you asking them to also walk in the light? As sunflowers naturally face the sun do you likewise face the Son?

Prayer: *Father, we come to you and ask you to nudge us to see others as you see them. When we are observed by others may we reflect your light to all. Amen*

Tapestry

Therefore, my beloved, as you have always obeyed, so now, not only in my presence but much more in my absence, work out your own salvation with fear and trembling, 13 for it is God who works in you, both to will and to work for his good pleasure.

Philippians 2:12-13

Tapestry is a heavy hand worked fabric with designs formed by threads inserted over and under the warp. It is commonly used as a wall hanging or perhaps used as a chair seat upholstery.

In life, our story can be compared to a tapestry which is what has happened to us and how we have responded. As we look back upon our lives we can see an unfinished tapestry which is totally unique to each one of us. It is only our story and does not reflect the actions of others in our lives.

So where are you in you in your story? Can you see in your tapestry how God has allowed circumstances to occur that were difficult for you to bear? Perhaps illness, death of a close friend, death of a family member, financial problems, marital failure unemployment etc.

How did you respond to the difficulties? Have you grown through the problems of life and now have a closer relationship with God? Perhaps you are angry with God for the hand you have been dealt.

It is one of life's severest lessons to realize that we are not the captains of our destinies, but we exist in an environment with God as our all in all.

As you look back on your tapestry everything was just great until_____.
(You fill in the blank). Perhaps the tapestry is too painful to look at.

Regardless of your response, God is with you as you add more threads of life to the design of your tapestry. God loves you and his mercy is available to you for forgiveness or healing. We are urged to work out our own futures with fear and trembling. In the process, God has permitted challenges to enter each one of our lives so that we can rely more completely on God.

God is standing at the door of your life. His arms are open and he will walk with you through the rest of your journey. As you evaluate your tapestry, in the future may it show the light of your positive relationship with your God.

Prayer:
Father, from this day forward, I'll walk closer to you in all of my journey. Thank you for the memories in the tapestry. I anticipate my future with you will be "Just a Closer Walk". Amen

Saying "Thank You"

You are the salt of the earth, but if the salt has lost its taste, how shall the saltiness be restored? It is no longer good for anything except to be thrown out and trampled under people's feet.
14 You are the light of the world. A city set on a hill cannot be hidden. 15 Nor do people light a lamp and put it under a basket, but on a stand, and it gives light to all in the house. 16 In the same way let your light shine before others, so that they may see your good works and give glory to your Father who is in heaven.
Matthew 5:13-16

Handwritten thank you notes are not used often enough. Most of our 'thank yous' are verbal if at all. Text 'thank yous' are probably the most common and pass the test of good manners for how to convey our gratitude. However, when I receive a handwritten 'thank you' note it really warms my heart because it resonates as being really very genuine and well thought out.

David, the psalmist was a master at saying "thanks to God". Take some time and read through the psalms and you will be left with a most positive heart that considers thanksgiving.

What in your life do you really take for granted? It's easy to not really pay attention to those in our lives that make our living more comfortable and pleasing but we seldom say thank you. We take those household chores of cooking, cleaning, ironing, and childcare for granted.

On a more in depth note, are we perhaps taking our salvation for granted? We need to be living a life of gratitude for that wonderful gift of God's grace. How about taking a time of personal assessment and consider writing a thank you note to God for his loving care for us in our temporal lives and especially our eternal destination? Don't let your thanks be private. We are the light of the world and our 'thank you', filled life needs to be shared.

Prayer:
Add your 'thank you' prayer here!

The Great Commission

And Jesus came and said to them, All authority in heaven and earth has been given to me. 19 Go therefore and make disciples of all nations, baptizing them in the name of he Father and of the Son and of the Holy Spirit, 20 teaching them to observe all that I have commanded you. And behold, I am with you always to the end of the age."

Matthew 28:18-20

We often ask at the time of visitation associated with one's passing "were there any last words"? The intent of the question is that when there are last words they can be remembered, savored and passed on to others. The significance of "last words" is associated with the ultimate level of importance on the mind of those soon to enter glory.

The last words of Jesus have been valued and remembered as "The Great Commission". Basically, Jesus is saying to his chosen disciples to "go and make disciples" as the most important directive of their individual ministries after Jesus rises into the clouds.

I must confess that my own "take" on going and making disciples was specifically aimed at missionaries. Being a member of a mission minded church, I gave money and offered prayers for missionaries supported by our church. Job done right" No! No! No!. The making of disciples cannot be so lightly compartmentalized.

My train of thought was that it is enough to confess Jesus as my Lord and Savior thereby making my own eternal salvation secure. However, Jesus never offered an option to those who just want to be "good enough".

Jesus last words to go and make disciples was not just meant for his present disciples. It was meant for all claiming to be his disciples. So, what does it mean to be included into the disciple category?

Perhaps a bit of introspection is fitting at this juncture. Let's consider that we are present with Jesus at the "Last Breakfast". Jesus is on the shore and is frying fish as a breakfast to the disciples who are returning from a night of unsuccessful fishing. It is at this "staff meeting" that Jesus singles Peter out and invites him to go for a walk. However, Jesus is inviting each of us to go for a similar walk. The conversation is identical in that Jesus is repeatedly asking each one of us if we really love him. Perhaps this isn't the first such conversation that you have had with Jesus or maybe you didn't recognize the significance of Jesus asking, "do you love me'?

What times of having a one-on-one conversation with Jesus do you recall? Was it the time of getting your education when Jesus wanted to know how you were going to honor him and make disciples with your education? Or was it in the accumulation stage of your life's journey? The time of gaining the perfect house, cottage, boat, auto etc? Do you remember the question "do you love me more than these"? The opportunities to give to kingdom causes to alleviate hunger, to make disciples etc. Do you remember? Lovest thou me? The walk with Jesus continues and he asks again "Lovest thou me"?

The final question Jesus asks is when both of them are seated taking a rest from the walk is, "lovest thou me more than these"? It's time to take a measure of where you are in relation to your family, possessions, relationships etc. "Do you love me more than these"? *End of walk.*

Prayer: *Father I confess my attitude to not listening when you were talking and questioning my intent and my level of devotion to you. Lord, I love you more than these. Amen*

The Quiet Majority

5 "If anyone sins in that he hears a public adjuration to testify, and though he is a witness, whether he has seen or come to know the matter, yet does not speak, he shall bear his iniquity;

Leviticus 5:1

12 Let no one despise you for your youth, but set the believers an example in speech, in conduct, in love, in faith, in purity.

I Timothy 4:12

Shyness or reticence to speak is not an adequate reason for remaining quiet when as a Christian it is an appropriate time to speak.

We can all remember those times when we spoke or blurted out something that was totally inappropriate, such as "when are you due"? The response being" I'm not due and have no future plans of bringing new life into the world". This is a time when words are inadequate to properly apologize for the faux pas. It's like trying to unring a bell. (Personal confession)

In the meditation for today, we are all encouraged/commanded to speak up when we have knowledge of a topic and know that our testimony will add clarity. This is not to be mistaken for gossip which is usually hearsay and intended to draw attention to the gossiper because of their magnificent fund of chatty information.

The rule for when it is appropriate and necessary to speak has not been written. However, within each of us is a voice or conscience which prompts us in the right direction. Yes, the Holy Spirit is very much a part of using us to speak and giving us the clarity of thinking and expression to give the utmost impact for our speech.

Do not be afraid of being "put down" by an obnoxious person who typically holds the floor with their verbose and endless authoritarian comments on almost every possible topic. Even though you fear ridicule by others, speak up and go on record where you stand and be biblically correct.

In America today it is time for the "silent majority" to step up to the plate and let the obtuse minority know that they are not the source of the correct opinions on all topics. Yes, America is on the cusp of a revival. This revival begins within each of us. Your input counts! Enough said!

Prayer: *Lord give me the courage and words to speak up for you every time the Spirit nudges me. Amen*

Turning the World Upside Down

*And Paul went in, as was his custom, and on three
Sabbath days he reasoned with them from the
scriptures, 3 explaining and proving that it was
necessary for the Christ to suffer and to rise from the
dead, and saying "This Jesus who I proclaim to you, is
the Christ."   4 And some of them were persuaded
and joined Paul and Silas, as did a great many of the
devout Greeks and not a few of the leading women. 5
But the Jews were jealous and taking some wicked men
of the rabble, they formed a mob, set the city in uproar,
and atacked the house of Jason, seeking to bring them
out to the crowd. 6 And when they could not find them,
they dragged Jason and some of the brothers before the
city authorities, shouting "these men who have turned
the world upside down have come here also---
Acts 17:2-6*

Paul and Silas in their visit to Thessalonica on
Paul's second missionary journey were doing their usual
preaching first to the Jews in their synagogue. The
listeners were mixed in their response. Some Greeks
were converted to the gospel, many of them were women.
Conversely, the Jews were upset with hearing the way of
salvation and they organized a mob of protesters. They
brought some of Paul's key people to the authorities with
the charge that these men have "turned the world upside
down".

Our society puts a great deal of emphasis upon
being "politically correct". We can count on being
accepted by all persons within our circle if we don't "step

on toes". It probably started in educational circles in the 70's. We wanted to make sure that we didn't "turn kids off". This movement gave rise to a counter movement toward charter schools, vouchers systems and public funding of Christian education in a few sectors.

However, our liberalization of educational philosophy was not new. Paul and Silas were evangelizing the Jews in Thessalonica who were charged the with "turning the world upside down.

The point of today's meditation is very obvious. Are we as Christians turning our environment "upside down for the gospel"? The question is how should we proceed:

- Being vocal for Jesus when the situation is ripe. Yes, we have the Holy Spirit within us that gives us an inner nudge to speak up.
- Helping others that need a ride, a visit, a meal brought in, a ride to the airport etc.
- A donation to a worthwhile agency.

Finally, we should be asking in our prayers to see others through the eyes of Jesus. Yes, each person is an image bearer of Jesus.

Prayer: *Father we want to "turn our world upside down" for you. Forgive our sins of being the quiet majority of politically correct people who seldom speak for you. Change our hearts to see others as you see them. Amen*

What If

*Just as day was breaking, Jesus stood on the shore; yet
the disciples did not know that it was Jesus. 5 Jesus
said to them, "Children, do you have any fish?" They
answered him, "no".6 He said to them "Cast the net on
the right side of the boat, and you will find some." So
they cast it and they were not able to haul it in, because
of the quantity of fish.7 That disciple whom Jesus loved
therefore said to Peter, "It is the Lord!"*
John 21 :4-7a

Each of us has had many situations in our lives that
caused us to wonder what the outcome would have been
if "what if" had taken place. Perhaps it was an automobile
accident, a fall, or an illness which has caused us to
wonder "what if" the outcome would have been had the
situation been slightly different.

In my personal life, I had an accident in my vehicle
where I crashed with a semi. Had it been slightly
different, my life would have probably been taken. As
you think back it is very probable that there have been
many "what ifs" that have taken place in your lives.

In today's scripture, Jesus appeared for the third
time to his disciples after his resurrection. What if Jesus
had not made the few post resurrection appearances to his

disciples, Mary Magdalene and the two travelers on the road to Emmaus?

Can it be assumed that the disciples would have returned to their previous vocations after the resurrection? Jesus appears on the shore of the Lake of Galilee and found the disciples fishing. Here Jesus proved his divine power in directing the disciples to fish on the other side of the boat and defying all odds their nets were filled with 153 large fish. Jesus cooked some of the fish and joined the disciples in eating the meal, further proving his spiritual and earthly natures. The verses that follow today's lesson further give validity to Jesus the great teacher having it out with Peter who had denied him three times to confess him three times.

It is safe to say that the entire beginning of Christianity rested upon Jesus' appearances after he was raised from the dead. Had Jesus not appeared we can assume that the inner urge to become missionaries would have fizzled on the shores of the Lake of Galilee and the disciples would have had discussions on the "what ifs" of Jesus death and resurrection.

When they had finished breakfast, Jesus said to Simon Peter, "Simon, son of John, do you love me more than these?" He said to him, "Yes, Lord; you know that I love you." He said to him, "Feed my lambs." 16 He said to him a second time, "Simon, son of John, do you love me?" He said to him, "Yes, Lord you know that I love you." He said to him, "Tend my sheep." 17 He said to him a third time, "Simon, son of John, do you love

me?" Peter was grieved because he said to him the third time, "Do you love me" and he said to him "Lord, you know everything; you know that I love you." Jesus said to him" Feed my sheep."
John 21:15-17

What if you suddenly realized that the "what ifs" in our lives were times when Jesus was trying to get our attention? As Jesus said to Peter, "feed my lambs" is probably what the "what ifs" in our lives were attempting to teach us.

Prayer: *Father as I think back upon the situations in my life that caused me to pause, may I further internalize that you were speaking and now I'm listening with an open mind and heart to be used by you for your kingdom. Amen*

What Really Matters

*19 "There was a rich man who was clothed in purple and
fine linen and who feasted sumptuously every
day. 20 And at his gate was laid a poor man named
Lazarus, covered with sores, 21 who desired to be fed
with what fell from the rich man's table. Moreover, even
the dogs came and licked his sores. 22 The poor man
died and was carried by the angels to Abraham's
side.[a] The rich man also died and was buried, 23 and
in Hades, being in torment, he lifted up his eyes
and saw Abraham far off and Lazarus at his side. 24 And
he called out, 'Father Abraham, have mercy on me, and
send Lazarus to dip the end of his finger in water
and cool my tongue, for I am in anguish in this flame.'
Luke:16:19-24*

Riches really matter in today's society. It totally
determines our lifestyle and our public status. Only the
very wealthy are looked up to for their excellence in
judgement. Governing boards of public and private
institutions require their trustees to have portfolios
bulging with great resources. We are surrounded by the
wealthy making decisions for colleges and nonprofits
that rely upon tuition and/or donations to maintain their
bottom line that guarantees their continued existence.

The parable of the rich man and Lazarus speaks of
lessons for all of us regardless of our retained wealth.
Lazarus led a miserable life on earth and actually lived

on the meager crumbs that fell off of the rich man's table. Note that when he died, he went directly to heaven where he joined other believers that were already in heaven. By contrast, the rich man who lived a sumptuous life here on earth when he died, went immediately to Hades, a place of continual torment. His buying days were over and his earthly disregard for others was receiving the ultimate in negative accolades in Hades.

A lesson to be learned from this parable is that earthly wealth has zero status in eternity. However, earthly stewardship of monies bears a positive reward.

Another lesson is that once death opens the door to our eternal reward, all negotiation ceases. All tests of one's life have been graded and eternal assignments are determined. No more grace is allocated for one's earthly actions.

Last lesson, Jesus taught many eternal lessons via parables. Jesus never spoke in a flippant manner and so our lessons to be learned were always totally applicable to the lives of those who heard them or read about them in the Bible. In light of Jesus' words for us today, it's time for personal introspection of our eternal bottom line. So, let's forget our net worth and concentrate on our spiritual bottom line.

Prayer: *Help us, Dear God, to be aware of the needs around us. Help us to recognize these needs and give us the courage to help people in need. Amen*

When You Pray

7 The end of all things is at hand; therefore be self-controlled and sober-minded for the sake of your prayers. 8 Above all, keep loving one another earnestly, since love covers a multitude of sins. 9 Show hospitality to one another without grumbling. 10 As each has received a gift, use it to serve one another, as good stewards of God's varied grace: 11 whoever speaks, as one who speaks oracles of God; whoever serves, as one who serves by the strength God supplies-in order that everything God may be glorified through Jesus Christ. To him belong glory and dominion forever and ever,
Amen
1 Peter 4:7-11

One of my favorite pastors, the late Warren Burgess, was very consistent in his counseling of struggling Christians. He never failed to ask if there was any issue in their lives which hindered their prayer lives. The question was aimed directly at getting an honest response as to where the person's relationship with Jesus was situated. It was most interesting to me as an elder listening to the conversation that there never was a question regarding what was meant by the question. It was aimed directly at one's relationship with Jesus.

The lives of Christians are never without challenges and difficulties for extended periods of time. All of us, upon occasion, face difficulties such as illness, marital speed bumps, financial challenges, temptations, dealing with addictions etc.

Many of us over the years have tried to be accepted by our secular friends and fellow Christians. This is a spiritual balance beam when we vie for the acceptance of both ends of the balance beam.

When we attempt to "be all things to all people", we are walking on the edge of hypocrisy. Others viewing our behavior might judge us as weak Christians who are quite faithful in weekly church attendance, but we change into a secular mode during the remainder of the week.

A very dear friend of mine has a huge painting on the wall directly behind his desk for all to see. It says, "I'm not ashamed of the gospel because it is the power of God for the salvation of everyone who believes". Romans 1:16a When sitting in his office it hit me that here is a man who walks with God. My friend is clear minded, self-controlled and loves Jesus.

To be clear-minded and self-controlled doesn't mean that we are sinless but that our lives are open to full disclosure when praying to our heavenly father. Where are you in your prayer life? Are there any areas that we just aren't comfortable with sharing with our God? Our heavenly father already knows if we are not open in our prayers. It's time to open up and feel the security of no barriers between us and God.

Prayer: *Father I confess that at times I've been trying too hard to be loved by all that I became as one who could not pray without my conscience bothering me and also it was impossible to share my hope of eternal life with my secular friends. Forgive me and help me to be open with you and with all my friends. Amen*

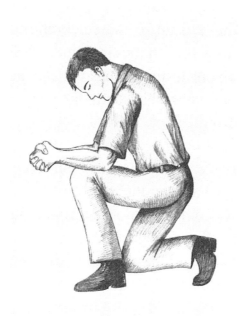

When Your Children Ask You

And these words that I command you today shall be on your heart. 7 You shall teach them diligently to your children and shall talk of them when you sit in your house, and when you walk by the way, and when you lie down, and when you rise.
Deuteronomy 6:6-7

When your children ask you what the Passover means and what led up to the celebration of the same, how will you as a Jewish parent respond? Such were the questions pertinent to the homes of later generations of those whose ancestors had actually been a part of the great exodus from Egypt.

In today's society, the questions to parents might center around what was the world like when you were growing up? Common responses might state that color TV was just being marketed, later came the deluge of cell phones, I pads, miniaturization of computers and increasing popularity of air travel.

A Christian home might pose some more probing questions such as how was the holocaust different from the abortions which are taking the lives of over 40,000 unborn babies in the USA annually? Another question might be what would the Christian world look if

288

everyone claiming to be believers would tithe 10% as depicted in the bible instead of the 3% as is the current percentage? As the family matures and there is a significant other in the life of a young adult just leaving the home of mom and dad, announcing we are going to be living together to see is we are really compatible. After all, everyone is doing it.

The real underlying question in many modern American homes is have you allocated time in your home to answer the questions of maturing children? Today's fast pace of dual income families, travel teams, sports on a school level beginning in middle school and through college etc. There is truly no time left for families to answer the questions that our children have, like discussions over a shared meal together.

Perhaps, we as parents and grandparents need to recognize that we have very few opportunities to speak to the conundrums facing our maturing families. How about making time for a special lunch out, a coke date or whatever just for a time of caring and bonding?

May God bless you in this very difficult time in your lives as parents and role models.

Prayer: Father, words can't express how I need you to relate to my family. Amen

.

Who Speaks for God?

Stephen renders a classic sermon to the Hellenistic Jews (Greek speaking). Stephen was one of the first seven deacons chosen in the early church to attend to the material needs of the widows. The selection of the first seven deacons was absolutely necessary so that the apostles would have adequate time for teaching, healing and conducting worship. Stephen also did wonders and signs which demonstrated his Spirit led actions.

Stephen's speech was met with criticism and false accusations from the Jews. He was dragged before the Sanhedrin for the filing of charges. It should be noted that Stephen's charge of blasphemy was the same charge that Jesus had faced. His speech before the Sanhedrin reflected Old Testament history and stopped just short of accusing the Jews of rejecting Jesus as the Messiah.

Stephen's speech is similar to that of the late Billy Graham, America's pastor. The similarities are that both Graham and Stephen each spoke the truth and spoke it with clarity.
Stephen was an evangelist at the beginning of the gospel being proclaimed and Billy Graham proclaimed the same gospel to thousands many years later, but the gospel didn't change.

It is natural to assume that if you are reading this devotional that you know what biblical preaching is. Many churches today are preaching a watered-down message. Sunday sermons are crafted to be politically correct. After all, the basic gospel might offend some listeners. I urge you to attend a church that does proclaim a message that is biblically sound.

Paul sums up the thinking regarding the unvarnished truth in Galatians:

But even if we or an angel from heaven should preach to you a gospel contrary to the one we preached to you, let him be accursed. 9 As we have said before, so now I say again: if anyone is preaching to you a gospel contrary to the one you received, let him be accursed. 10 For am I now seeking the approval of man, or of God? Or am I trying to please man? If I were still trying to please man, I would not be a servant of Christ.
Galatians: 1:8-10

Prayer: Father I need to evaluate where I worship and how my children are being educated in our present church. This is a decision that I am praying and reading about. Help me to lead my family with your blessing.
In Jesus name, Amen

Why Me, Lord?

*In the course of time Cain brought to the Lord an
offering of the fruit of the ground, 4 and Abel also
bought of the firstborn of his flock and of the fat
portions. And the Lord had regard for Abel and his
offering, 5 but for Cain and his offering he had no
regard. So Cain was very angry and his face fell.*
Genesis 4:3-5

Cain must have thought "why me, Lord" when
God did not find favor with his offering of his harvest.
Insane jealously took over his psyche when he observed
that God found favor with his brother's offering of the
finest of his flock. After all, he gave as much as was
expected. Certainly, God is picking on me must have
been a thought he harbored.

We do know that God is totally aware of our
motivation in or relationship with the Almighty. Personal
introspection of our motives in our relationship with God
is mind blowing in that God knows our hearts more
clearly than what we care to admit. God sees the real core
of our being with all the veneer layers removed.

Cain paid the price in that he was shunned by his
peers, had diminished crop yields, and above all was not
at peace with God. What a way to exist! Being out of
favor with God must be at the very heart of a depressed
spiritual life.

Where are you at in your relationship with God? Are you at peace? Or are you attempting to negotiate in your thoughts as to how much is enough? <u>God wants your all, not just part.</u> When you cross the line of total submission, a peace beyond description will come over you.

Prayer: I need you every hour and in all my responses of saying thanks for your plan of salvation. Amen

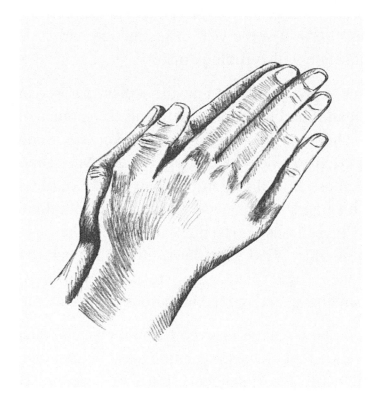

Author Biography

Chuck's roots are in Redlands, California. It was a time before smog. Redlands was the navel orange capital of the USA. A truly beautiful location which featured a backdrop of mountains that were snow covered for most of the year.

Calvin College (University) was the place of college training. 1958 was the year of graduation with a degree in Education with a Biology major.

Sharon Wickstra became the reason for staying in Michigan. She became my wife and the mother of our three children. My oldest son, Mike was suddenly transported to Glory at the age of 23. My remaining children are still Michigan residents and have presented me with grandchildren and later great grandchildren. The family loves Jesus! I'm so blessed! In 2011 Sharon joined Mike in Glory. Two years later, Orlene Kuieck became my wife and filled the roles beautifully for companionship and mutual humorous "senior moments".

Two careers were in store for me. One in education with time spent in teaching, administration including the position of superintendent. Later, a second career involved group insurance programs that specialized in Michigan public schools. All my time in education and insurance were most enjoyable.

My church affiliation involved church officer duties of deacon, elder and administrative positions in Classis leadership. All the church related positions were with the Reformed Church in America.

Currently, retirement is my classification, but activity is still at a very fast gait of yard grooming, symphony attendance, and time in God's beautiful outdoors in a fishing boat and occasionally in a deer blind.

Chuck Porte

seaporte@sbcglobal.net

In The Net

Made in the USA
Monee, IL
14 September 2023

42672470R00164